KATIE COURIC

WOMEN of ACHIEVEMENT

KATIE COURIC

Sherry Beck Paprocki

CHELSEA HOUSE PUBLISHERS
PHILADELPHIA

Frontispiece: Katie Couric's warm, positive personality attracts millions of viewers to the *Today* show on NBC.

PRODUCED BY 21st Century Publishing and Communications, Inc., New York, N.Y.

Chelsea House Publishers
EDITOR IN CHIEF Sally Cheney
ASSOCIATE EDITOR IN CHIEF Kim Shinners
PRODUCTION MANAGER Pamela Loos
ART DIRECTOR Sara Davis
DIRECTOR OF PHOTOGRAPHY Judy L. Hasday
COVER DESIGNER Sara Davis

The Chelsea House World Wide Web address is
http://www.chelseahouse.com

First Printing
1 3 5 7 9 8 6 4 2

Library of Congress Cataloging-in-Publication Data

Paprocki, Sherry.
Katie Couric / by Sherry Beck Paprocki
    p.   cm. — (Women of achievement)
Includes bibliographical references and index.
ISBN 0-7910-5881-6 — ISBN 0-7910-5862-4 (pbk.)
1. Couric, Katie, 1957—Juvenile literature. 2. Television personalities—
United States—Biography—Juvenile literature. 3. Women television
personalities—United States—Biography—Juvenile literature. [1. Couric,
Katie, 1957– . 2. Television personalities. 3. Women—Biography.]
I. Title. II. Series.

PN1992.4.C68 P37 2000
791.45′028′092—dc21
[B]   00-060133

CONTENTS

WOMEN of ACHIEVEMENT

Jane Addams
SOCIAL WORKER

Madeleine Albright
STATESWOMAN

Marian Anderson
SINGER

Susan B. Anthony
WOMAN SUFFRAGIST

Clara Barton
AMERICAN RED CROSS FOUNDER

Margaret Bourke-White
PHOTOGRAPHER

Rachel Carson
BIOLOGIST AND AUTHOR

Cher
SINGER AND ACTRESS

Hillary Rodham Clinton
FIRST LADY AND ATTORNEY

Katie Couric
JOURNALIST

Diana, Princess of Wales
HUMANITARIAN

Emily Dickinson
POET

Elizabeth Dole
POLITICIAN

Amelia Earhart
AVIATOR

Gloria Estefan
SINGER

Jodie Foster
ACTRESS AND DIRECTOR

Betty Friedan
FEMINIST

Althea Gibson
TENNIS CHAMPION

Ruth Bader Ginsburg
SUPREME COURT JUSTICE

Helen Hayes
ACTRESS

Katharine Hepburn
ACTRESS

Mahalia Jackson
GOSPEL SINGER

Helen Keller
HUMANITARIAN

**Ann Landers/
Abigail Van Buren**
COLUMNISTS

Barbara McClintock
BIOLOGIST

Margaret Mead
ANTHROPOLOGIST

Edna St. Vincent Millay
POET

Julia Morgan
ARCHITECT

Toni Morrison
AUTHOR

Grandma Moses
PAINTER

Lucretia Mott
WOMAN SUFFRAGIST

Sandra Day O'Connor
SUPREME COURT JUSTICE

Rosie O'Donnell
ENTERTAINER AND COMEDIAN

Georgia O'Keeffe
PAINTER

Eleanor Roosevelt
DIPLOMAT AND HUMANITARIAN

Wilma Rudolph
CHAMPION ATHLETE

Elizabeth Cady Stanton
WOMAN SUFFRAGIST

Harriet Beecher Stowe
AUTHOR AND ABOLITIONIST

Barbra Streisand
ENTERTAINER

Elizabeth Taylor
ACTRESS AND ACTIVIST

Mother Teresa
HUMANITARIAN AND
RELIGIOUS LEADER

Barbara Walters
JOURNALIST

Edith Wharton
AUTHOR

Phillis Wheatley
POET

Oprah Winfrey
ENTERTAINER

Babe Didrikson Zaharias
CHAMPION ATHLETE

"REMEMBER THE LADIES"

MATINA S. HORNER

"Remember the Ladies." That is what Abigail Adams wrote to her husband John, then a delegate to the Continental Congress, as the Founding Fathers met in Philadelphia to form a new nation in March of 1776. "Be more generous and favorable to them than your ancestors. Do not put such unlimited power in the hands of the Husbands. If particular care and attention is not paid to the Ladies," Abigail Adams warned, "we are determined to foment a Rebellion, and will not hold ourselves bound by any Laws in which we have no voice, or Representation."

The words of Abigail Adams, one of the earliest American advocates of women's rights, were prophetic. Because when we have not "remembered the ladies," they have, by their words and deeds, reminded us so forcefully of the omission that we cannot fail to remember them. For the history of American women is as interesting and varied as the history of our nation as a whole. American women have played an integral part in founding, settling, and building our country. Some we remember as remarkable women who—against great odds—achieved distinction in the public arena: Anne Hutchinson, who in the 17th century became a charismatic religious leader; Phillis Wheatley, an 18th-century black slave who became a poet; Susan B. Anthony, whose name is synonymous with the 19th-century women's rights movement, and who led the struggle to enfranchise women; and in the 20th century, Amelia Earhart, the first woman to cross the Atlantic Ocean by air.

These extraordinary women certainly merit our admiration, but other women, "common women," many of them all but forgotten, should also be recognized for their contributions to American thought and culture. Women have been community builders; they have founded schools and formed voluntary associations to help those in need; they have assumed the major responsibility for rearing children, passing on from one generation to the next the values that keep a culture alive. These and innumerable other contributions, once ignored, are now being recognized by scholars, students, and the public. It is exciting and gratifying that a part of our history that was hardly acknowledged a few generations ago is now being studied and brought to light.

In recent decades, the field of women's history has grown from obscurity to a politically controversial splinter movement to academic respectability, in many cases mainstreamed into such traditional disciplines as history, economics, and psychology. Scholars of women, both female and male, have organized research centers at such prestigious institutions as Wellesley College, Stanford University, and the University of California. Other notable centers for women's studies are the Center for the American Woman and Politics at the Eagleton Institute of Politics at Rutgers University; the Henry A. Murray Research Center for the Study of Lives, at Radcliffe College; and the Women's Research and Education Institute, the research arm of the Congressional Caucus on Women's Issues. Other scholars and public figures have established archives and libraries, such as the Schlesinger Library on the History of Women in America, at Radcliffe College, and the Sophia Smith Collection, at Smith College, to collect and preserve the written and tangible legacies of women.

From the initial donation of the Women's Rights Collection in 1943, the Schlesinger Library grew to encompass vast collections documenting the manifold accomplishments of American women. Simultaneously, the women's movement in general and the academic discipline of women's studies in particular also began with a narrow definition and gradually expanded their mandate. Early causes, such as woman suffrage and social reform, abolition, and organized labor were joined by newer concerns, such as the history of women in business and the professions and in politics and government; the study of the family; and social issues such as health policy and education.

Women, as historian Arthur M. Schlesinger, jr., once pointed out, "have constituted the most spectacular casualty of traditional history. They have made up at least half the human race, but you could never tell that by looking at the books historians write." The new breed of historians is remedying that omission. They have written books about immigrant women and about working-class women who struggled for survival in cities and about black women who met the challenges of life in rural areas. They are telling the stories of women who, despite the barriers of tradition and economics, became lawyers and doctors and public figures.

The women's studies movement has also led scholars to question traditional interpretations of their respective disciplines. For example, the study of war has traditionally been an exercise in military and political analysis, an examination of strategies planned and executed by men. But scholars of women's history have pointed out that wars have also been periods of tremendous change and even opportunity for women, because the very absence of men on the home front enabled them to expand their educational, economic, and professional activities and to assume leadership in their homes.

The early scholars of women's history showed a unique brand of courage in choosing to investigate new subjects and take new approaches to old ones. Often, like their subjects, they endured criticism and even ostracism by their academic colleagues. But their efforts have unquestionably been worthwhile, because with the publication of each new study and book another piece of the historical patchwork is sewn into place, revealing an increasingly comprehensive picture of the role of women in our rich and varied history.

Such books on groups of women are essential, but books that focus on the lives of individuals are equally indispensable. Biographies can be inspirational, offering their readers the example of people with vision who have looked outside themselves for their goals and have often struggled against great obstacles to achieve them. Marian Anderson, for instance, had to overcome racial bigotry in order to perfect her art and perform as a concert singer. Isadora Duncan defied the rules of classical dance to find true artistic freedom. Jane Addams had to break down society's notions of the proper role for women in order to create new social situations, notably the settlement house. All of these women had to come to terms both with themselves and with the world in which they lived. Only then could they move ahead as pioneers in their chosen callings.

Biography can inspire not only by adulation but also by realism. It helps us to see not only the qualities in others that we hope to emulate, but also, perhaps, the weaknesses that made them "human." By helping us identify with the subject on a more personal level they help us feel that we, too, can achieve such goals. We read about Eleanor Roosevelt, for instance, who occupied a unique and seemingly enviable position as the wife of the president. Yet we can sympathize with her inner dilemma; an inherently shy woman, she had to force herself to live a most public life in order to use her position to benefit others. We may not be able to imagine ourselves having the immense poetic talent of Emily Dickinson, but from her story we can understand the challenges faced by a creative woman who was expected to fulfill many family responsibilities. And though few of us will ever reach the level of athletic accomplishment displayed by Wilma Rudolph or Babe Zaharias, we can still appreciate their spirit, their overwhelming will to excel.

A biography is a multifaceted lens. It is first of all a magnification, the intimate examination of one particular life. But at the same time, it is a wide-angle lens, informing us about the world in which the subject lived. We come away from reading about one life knowing more about the social, political, and economic fabric of the time. It is for this reason, perhaps, that the great New England essayist Ralph Waldo Emerson wrote in 1841, "There is properly no history: only biography." And it is also why biography, and particularly women's biography, will continue to fascinate writers and readers alike.

Katie Couric's career has been flying high ever since she got her big break and became host of the Today *show. Here she demonstrates the capabilities of the Parabounce on the show outside the studio at Rockefeller Center in New York City in 1999.*

1

FLYING HIGH

It was a nippy day outside the studios of NBC's *Today* show at Rockefeller Center in New York City. That did not stop the costumed crowd from gathering behind the ropes that divide the *Today* show hosts from the audience. Hundreds of people were crowded in the roped-off area that day, October 29, 1999. They hoped for an opportunity to talk to *Today* cohosts Katie Couric and Matt Lauer, weatherman Al Roker, and news reader Ann Curry.

"Has anybody seen Katie?" asked Lauer, who was dressed like the main character in the movie *Austin Powers* and could hardly talk because of the fake teeth in his mouth. Al Roker was dressed as Dr. Evil, and next to him stood the dark-haired Ann Curry in a Pocahontas outfit.

"Well, you know, you are a lovely Pocahontas. You are the perfect Dr. Evil. I put the grr in swinger, baby, but where is Katie?" asked Lauer.

Today coworkers feigned ignorance until Katie swooped down from the sky in a Peter Pan outfit complete with green leotards. As she dangled from a rope, she lightly kicked a member of the

French figure-skating heart-throb Philippe Candeloro presents Katie with roses following a performance on Today. *Katie has stolen the hearts of millions of viewers and receives credit for much of the program's success.*

audience in the head. Then the cord dropped her onto the pavement in front of the outdoor crowd. Katie laughed as she struggled to her feet.

"Hey! Smooth landing," called out Al Roker.

"You're not Wendy, Michael, and John," Katie replied, an innocent, wistful look crossing her face.

"I loved when you kicked that person in the head over there," Matt said.

Katie looked embarrassed. "I'm so sorry, did I hurt

you?" she asked, looking at the person she kicked. "We should have made sure all short people were standing over there."

It is a lighthearted segment on *Today*, the most popular early morning television show in America. Katie Couric is the pert cohost who, in her forties, earns one of the biggest salaries in the business. Just a few months before her Peter Pan appearance, Katie signed a new, four-year contract with NBC that promised her $7 million a year.

Experts say that Katie is the primary reason the *Today* show has the top morning ratings in the business, more than its biggest rival, *Good Morning America*, on ABC. Advertisers like Katie and Matt so much that they spend nearly half of their advertising budget for affiliate news programs during the *Today* show.

But Katie's popularity isn't simply due to scenes like the Halloween show in which she struggled through an acrobatic feat. Television viewers around the world have watched Katie Couric struggle in her life as well. In January 1998, she lost her husband, attorney Jay Monahan, when he died of colon cancer. Yet she returned to the *Today* show just a month after Jay's death and returned to the business of doing what she does best.

The broadcasting business came naturally to Katie. Her father was a print journalist, who advised his daughter that she would make more money by training for a career in broadcast journalism. But there were stumbling blocks along the way. She did not impress her bosses at first. Her perky look contrasted sharply with the more elegant appearance of news anchors of the time. Katie often thought that she did not look enough like a prom queen to get an anchor spot. At just under 5'4" tall, she was far from statuesque. Her bosses sometimes encouraged her to let her short hair grow longer or to wear soft, fluffy sweaters. Katie refused.

Eventually, Katie Couric found success on her own terms. Her down-to-earth style shows through on the program, and her personality is her biggest attribute. She has the ability to make her interviewees feel at ease. Many of her subjects have been surprised by her finesse—some of them have said things during a Katie Couric interview that they may not have said anywhere else.

Frequently, Katie's difficult questions catch people off guard. In 1992 she asked tough questions of presidential candidates. Among them was Republican hopeful Pat Buchanan, who at the time of the interview had already lost to President George Bush in primary elections in several states. Katie demanded to know why Buchanan was still staying in the race: "Are you trying to drive the President crazy, or are you just on a big ego trip?" she asked.

Katie admits that she seems pushy at times during interviews, but she doesn't want to be too obnoxious. "My only real concern while I'm being provocative and while I'm challenging an interview subject is that I'm being fair," she once told a writer for the *Saturday Evening Post.*

That same year she took on another presidential candidate. This time it was the Reform Party candidate, the outspoken Ross Perot, whom she pressed for answers about specific issues. A surprised Perot retaliated by asking Katie if she was "trying to prove her manhood."

During the 1996 presidential campaign, Republican candidate Bob Dole and his wife, Elizabeth, appeared on a segment of the *Today* show. The two wanted to talk about a book they had written about their marriage. But Katie had other ideas. She asked Bob Dole about the funding he had received from the tobacco industry and the comments that he had made during the campaign that appeared to apologize for the cancer caused by the industry. Dole chose to avoid Katie's question

and instead verbally attacked her for her media bias.

Many Republicans blamed that episode for a subsequent decrease in Dole's popularity. After Katie's interview, other reporters continued to question Dole about his apparent loyalty to the tobacco industry. At the end of the campaign, Elizabeth Dole returned to the television show. During the interview, she talked so fervently about her husband's agenda that Katie could hardly ask any questions. It was as if Mrs. Dole was trying to keep Katie from talking at all. "Geez," the *Today* show cohost said in front of millions of viewers. "It's hard to get a word in edgewise with you, Mrs. Dole."

That's Katie Couric at her best. She will take a formal interview that would make many broadcasters tense and make a down-to-earth comment that leaves

Republican presidential nominee Bob Dole (right) and his wife, Elizabeth (left), appeared on the Today *show during the 1996 campaign. Many Republicans blamed their candidate's responses to Katie's tough questions for his subsequent drop in popularity.*

10 million people around the world chuckling. Television viewers appreciate this approach to handling interviews.

The *Today* show is much more than interviews with politicians, however. It mixes light segments, such as the Halloween episode, with an equal portion of serious, hard news. Katie enjoys talking about flowers and vegetables with gardening contributor Rebecca Cole during one segment as much as she enjoys tossing tough questions at world leaders in another. She rides around Hollywood in a limo with comedian Jerry Seinfeld as comfortably as she covers a presidential candidate on the road.

Katie does not shy away from either kind of story. And her persistence and determination to handle difficult interviews has paid off.

One such interview took place in 1997, when Katie attempted to meet with Yasir Arafat, a Palestinian leader, who was visiting Washington, D.C. The producers of *Today* had allotted three minutes and 50 seconds for the meeting. Katie planned to tape the interview the day before it aired, so she and three camera crews took a flight to Washington, D.C., to meet Arafat. But when Katie arrived at the Ritz-Carlton, where Arafat was staying, she learned that the interview was postponed. Finally Arafat appeared and said he was too tired from his trip from the Middle East to participate.

Katie was irked, but that didn't stop her from trying to get the interview. Before she left the hotel she extracted a promise from Arafat that he would meet her the next day in New York. Katie flew back home, hopeful that Arafat would keep his word.

The next morning she arrived at the *Today* show still perturbed from the events of the day before. A few hours after the *Today* show broadcast ended, she received a telephone call. Arafat agreed to meet with Katie at 6:15 that evening. Again, NBC's film crews

were alerted and the interview was scheduled. But a few hours later, Arafat's people called again. He would be unavailable until 9:15 that night, when he would meet her at the United Nations Plaza.

Katie's bosses were ready to give up and suggested that she cancel the meeting. But Katie refused. She remained determined to clinch the interview.

Before going to the United Nations Plaza, Katie stopped by an NBC party for a short time, then got back to her car. While the driver took her to the United Nations, she studied her notes for the Arafat interview. She found the 29th floor of the UN building swarming with security provided by both Arafat's people and by the U.S. State Department. The New York City Police Department had people roaming around, too.

Katie refuses to take herself too seriously, a fact that endears her to her legions of fans. Above, she shows off an ensemble fit for a '50s prom queen while appearing on the 500th episode of The Rosie O'Donnell Show. *Laughing with her are (from left) Wynonna Judd, Bette Midler, and Rosie.*

Katie, shown interviewing President Bill Clinton at the White House in 1999, insists on asking tough questions and tackling hard issues.

Even though she had been up since nearly 4:45 that morning, Katie was wide awake for her 9:15 interview with Arafat that night. She finally conducted the session in a studio set up in a room near the area where Arafat was staying. Yasir Arafat learned that Katie asks hard questions. A *George* magazine reporter, who had been waiting in a nearby room, recalled hearing Arafat get angry during the interview. In response to questions about some Middle East conflicts, the Palestinian leader shouted, "Lies! Big lies. . . . Ask your government to give you the truth!" But at the end of the interview, after the cameras were off, Arafat apologized for his tirade. "Hey, that's OK," said Katie. "I can take it."

Through the years, the *Today* show cohost has taken quite a lot. Still, she continues to give a lot back and remains famous for catching people off guard in her interviews. Moments like the one where she chastised

Elizabeth Dole have defined Katie's career on the *Today* show. Her quick wit and big grin have drawn viewers since she was named a cohost of the show in 1991. The ratings have been rising ever since.

On the *Today* show, Katie has given the impression to viewers that they are peeking in on the neighbors next door. She easily mixes the show's soft features with hard news and always delivers her toughest questions with her trademark smile. She has a broad range of interests, but readily admits—even on the air—that some things do not interest her at all.

During one *Today* show segment, Bryant Gumbel was talking with sportscaster Joe Garagiola about football statistics. Katie finally covered her face and yelled, "Okay, okay, I can't even pretend that I understand it!"

Viewers give constant feedback on their feelings about *Today,* and Katie's bosses at NBC value her reputation. During the spring and summer of 1999, there were rumors that Katie would leave the *Today* show. Instead her bosses made an offer that she could not refuse: $28 million spread out over the next four years.

With the death of her husband, Katie developed a newfound understanding and compassion for people who have, like herself, suffered great loss. Because Katie is a woman immersed in a top-flight career, it does not seem unusual that she would be seen flying through the air at Rockefeller Center. But maybe she should be dressed as Superwoman rather than Peter Pan.

By the time Katie was a senior in high school, she possessed the ability to put people at ease, a gift that would become extremely important when she started her career as a journalist.

2

BORN TO CHAT

Katherine Anne Couric was born January 7, 1957, the youngest of John and Elinor Couric's four children. When she was born, her oldest sister, Emily, was already 10 years old. Next came Clara, nicknamed Kiki, and finally John. The family lived in Arlington, Virginia, a historic suburb of Washington, D.C.

When Katie was six months old, the Courics moved into a large, four-bedroom brick house with a neat front lawn and flowering crab apple trees that bloomed in the spring. On warm summer days, the Couric kids played for hours outside with other neighborhood children.

Katie's love for journalism probably came from the years her father spent in the business. John Couric was an associate news editor with United Press International, a news service that provided articles to newspapers around the world. Later he became a successful public relations executive in the Washington, D.C., area. After retirement he taught for a while at the University of Maryland.

Katie's mother, Elinor, kept busy rearing her four children and

Born in a suburb of Washington, D.C., Katie Couric often saw the landmarks of the city, such as the Capitol Building. She grew up learning about the news business from her father, an associate news editor with United Press International.

volunteering where her help was needed, including at the local Planned Parenthood center. One of her favorite hobbies was arranging bouquets of flowers. When Katie was older, her mother took a job at the clothing store Lord and Taylor.

Both of Katie's parents grew up in the 1930s, during the Great Depression, a time of great economic hardship in the United States. As a result both were careful about spending money. Even so, Katie and her siblings had a comfortable childhood and faced few problems.

As the youngest, Katie always strived to find a niche for herself, possibly because her two older sisters and older brother seemed to overshadow her much of the time. She became the precocious little sister full of wit and humor. Young Katie was fun to be around, and entertaining as well. "Even when she was an infant, we'd put her in her plastic seat and then all sit around and watch her," Emily recalled years later while talking to *Good Housekeeping* magazine.

All was not entertainment in the Couric family, though. John and Elinor Couric stressed the importance of schoolwork. At dinner, each child would bring a new vocabulary word to the table to share with everyone else. Katie, of course, was not left out of this game.

By the time she started first grade at Jamestown Elementary, Katie was already a student who stood out from the crowd. "When her parents came for conferences, I couldn't think of anything bad to say," her first-grade teacher once told a reporter from the *Washington Post*. "She had the sweetest smile you could imagine and absolutely the best handwriting."

One by one, Katie watched her brother and sisters grow up and become more independent. That meant they had less time for her. But as she grew older, the youngest member of the family still found ways to fit into her siblings' lives. By the time she was 10 years old, she had memorized the names of the students in her sisters' high school yearbooks. She would walk up to those older students when she saw them in public and call them by name. This special talent made Katie popular with her schoolmates. During her final year at Jamestown Elementary she was elected the student body president.

Although Katie was an organizer and a socializer, classmates also knew there were surprises when Katie was around. She had a reputation as the class comedian. "I was a real clown who goofed off a lot," she once told *Working Mother* magazine.

Katie's teenage years were carefree. Sometimes in the summers she and her friends lightened their hair and tossed water balloons at people on the beach. In the winters, they ice skated and attended parties at each other's homes.

Katie had an outgoing personality and enjoyed being the center of attention. At Yorktown High School in Arlington, Virginia, she gained a reputation for being friendly and took part in many activities. Somewhat athletic, Katie participated in track and field as well as in gymnastics. She also followed her two sisters into cheerleading. Katie once said that the worst thing that ever happened to her in high school was not being named captain of the cheerleading squad.

Although a good student, Katie was also a procrastinator who liked to wait until deadlines to finish most of her school projects. She managed to meet those deadlines, and her teachers voted her into the National Honor Society. Another favorite activity was writing for the school newspaper. Like her father, Katie always liked to write, and she was good at it. It wasn't unusual for her teachers to read her essays aloud in front of the class.

Katie liked being around other students and working with those younger than she. After finishing her freshman year of high school, she became a counselor for the Columbia Lighthouse for the Blind Day Camp in Washington, D.C. Katie's parents encouraged her to apply for the nonpaying job so that she would learn the importance of helping others who were less fortunate.

That summer Katie was responsible for eight campers who were four or five years old. The group liked music a lot. The first-time counselor recalled later that she sometimes would play "The Entertainer" on the piano, while one little boy in the group stood up and rocked his head back and forth in time to the music. Another camper always sang "Lean on Me" at the top of his lungs.

Once Katie took her students with a group of other campers on a field trip to the National Air and Space Museum near the U.S. Capitol Building in Washington.

Katie's life at high school was mostly trouble-free. A well-rounded student, she belonged to the National Honor Society and competed in athletic events such as gymnastics and track and field. Like her two older sisters, Katie also joined the cheerleading squad.

At the museum, one of Katie's charges, a little girl named Carolyn, screamed because she was afraid to ride the escalator. With patience and understanding, Katie reassured the frightened child that the escalator was safe, and she helped Carolyn learn to ride the motorized stairs.

Many years later Katie wrote a short article for *Reader's Digest*, in which she explained how that experience affected her career. "Working my way up through reporting jobs . . . I found that—as in my experience with Carolyn and the escalator—I had developed an ability to put folks at ease and make them feel comfortable during even the most potentially contentious interviews. I acquired this ability by learning to be a patient, sympathetic listener at the Lighthouse camp."

Just once during high school, Katie got into serious trouble when she was caught holding a cigarette in the girls' bathroom. Although she claimed that she was holding the cigarette for a friend, she was briefly suspended from school for the offense.

Weeks before her graduation from high school, Katie attended the senior prom with her boyfriend. The couple decided to be adventuresome in their choice of clothing. Katie wore a long, white dress and thought she looked quite glamorous. Her boyfriend wore a white tuxedo, a white top hat, and carried a white cane. "At the time we thought we looked fabulous, but now I look at those pictures and want to kill myself," Katie told a reporter from *People* magazine who was writing a story about celebrities and their proms.

By the time she graduated from Yorktown High in the spring of 1975, Katie had decided to attend the University of Virginia (UVa) the next fall. Located in Charlottesville, not far from the Atlantic Ocean, UVa is considered one of the best colleges in Katie's home state of Virginia. From Arlington, she had to travel a few hours to get there.

In college Katie was as active and as well liked as she had been in high school. She became an associate editor of the *Cavalier Daily* newspaper on campus. She also joined the Delta Delta Delta sorority, but made friends both inside and outside of the sorority. At UVa Katie took courses in journalism, as well as many other subjects. Her interest in the news business continued to grow during her college years.

During the summers Katie volunteered at radio

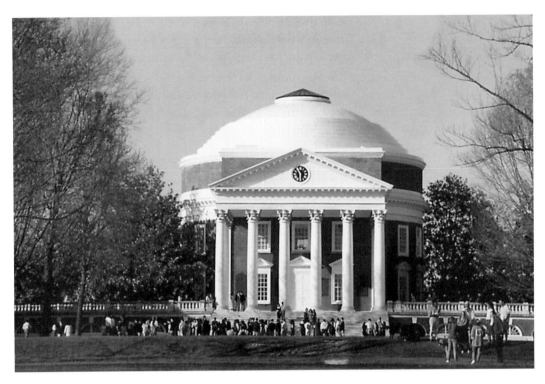

stations, where she learned how to conduct interviews. On the advice of her father, she chose broadcasting as her career. Katie's parents encouraged all of their children to be whatever they wanted to be, but they were never too pushy when it came to the kids' chosen professions. The Courics wanted each of their children to find an enjoyable career. Katie was the only one to choose the news business. Emily started out as a high school science teacher, then served on the Charlottesville, Virginia, board of education, and later ran for a seat in the Virginia State Senate. Katie's other sister, Kiki, chose to become a landscape architect in Boston. Their brother, John, became an accountant.

By the time Katie graduated with honors from the University of Virginia in 1979, she knew she had to strike out on a career of her own.

Katie enjoyed her years at the University of Virginia (above), where she maintained excellent grades, worked on the school newspaper, and joined a sorority.

When Katie first entered the news business, no one expected her to be a star. "I think that [attitude] really helped me," she observed later. "It forced me to work."

3

UPS AND DOWNS IN THE NEWS BUSINESS

I n the late 1970s, jobs were hard to find in the broadcasting field. But Katie had some skills that worked in her favor. She was ambitious, confident, and competitive. And she also knew a few people in the business. Katie was optimistic that she could get what she wanted in life.

All of the major television networks—CBS, NBC, and ABC—had their central offices in New York City. But they also had smaller, satellite offices in Washington, D.C. After all, the nation's capital is the scene for many news stories. Katie wanted to work where these big decisions were made. The youngest Couric got her foot in the door at the ABC News Washington bureau partly because of her sister Kiki.

One day Katie walked into the offices of the ABC News Washington bureau. She managed to talk the security guard into putting her on the phone with a man who was the executive producer in charge of a program called *World News Tonight*. "I said, 'Hi, Davey, this is Katie Couric, you don't know me, but my sister Kiki went to Yorktown [High School] with Steve and Eddie, your twin brothers. Do you think I could come up?'" Katie later recalled her words in an interview with *Good Housekeeping* magazine.

The young job seeker was hired for a minor position as a desk assistant. Her job was not boring, though. Some of ABC's top news personalities worked there. Sam Donaldson, one of the up-and-coming newscasters of the time who then covered the White House for ABC, gave her a grand welcome. On her first day at work, he asked Katie her name. When she told him, he jumped on her desk and started singing it aloud. Then Donaldson invited her to join him for a White House briefing. Katie could hardly believe it. It was her first day on the job and she was on her way to the White House.

But Katie's stay at ABC did not last long. Less than a year after she started her job, the ABC News Washington bureau chief moved to Cable News Network (CNN), which is based in Atlanta, Georgia. A new television network just founded by Georgia native Ted Turner, CNN was hiring newscasters from other top networks in the country. When the ABC News chief decided to take some of his staff members to the new CNN Washington bureau with him, Katie and her friend Wendy Walker, were among them.

With the move to CNN, Katie received a promotion to become an assignment editor. She would dish out ideas to reporters and tell them which stories needed to be covered each day. As part of her work, Katie occasionally appeared on television. But her high-pitched voice was not well suited to the airwaves. It nearly squeaked when she was on the air.

Katie wasn't an immediate television success by any means. In addition to the problem with her voice, she looked unusually young. Television executives thought that viewers would not accept serious news reports from someone who appeared to be inexperienced. One time while she was on the air, newscasters at the

CNN Washington bureau received a call from the network president, Reese Schonfeld. He reportedly issued a command, "I never want to see her on the air again."

Katie was concerned that Schonfeld had dashed her hopes for a career as a broadcast reporter. Yet she knew she needed to work hard on her presentation if she wanted to fulfill her dream. "I stunk," she told a *Newsweek* reporter years later. "I had nobody on my way up saying, 'We're going to make you a star,' and I think that really helped me. It forced me to work."

The young woman did not give up. When the

In the early 1980s, Katie seized the opportunity to move to Atlanta, Georgia, and produce the CNN program Take Two.

When CNN president Reese Schonfeld (right) first heard Katie Couric on television, he reportedly ordered, "I never want to see her on the air again."

opportunity came in the early 1980s, she moved to Atlanta to become the producer of *Take Two*, a CNN program that was coanchored by the husband-and-wife team of Don Farmer and Chris Curle. A news and information show, *Take Two* aired two hours daily. As a producer, Katie helped the anchors organize the show and pull together the information it presented.

Farmer and Curle liked Katie very much and thought the young producer deserved more opportunities. Occasionally, they allowed her to go on the air as part of their program. While she was in Atlanta,

Katie took lessons with a voice trainer to improve her on-air presentation. The lessons seemed to help, and Katie soon began projecting her voice better over the airwaves. Her on-air interviewing and reporting styles also improved. Eventually she was given the position of a full-time correspondent for the show.

By 1982 Katie had gained some much needed experience in the broadcast business. When Farmer and Curle decided to do a live broadcast in Cuba, they took Katie along to produce the three-hour program, which was based at an old hotel in Havana. Katie did quite a bit of research while she was in Cuba, and she managed, in very broken Spanish, to direct the television technicians throughout the live program.

After returning from Cuba, Katie accepted a new position with CNN as a political correspondent. During 1984 she covered the presidential elections in which the Democratic candidate, Walter Mondale, opposed the Republican candidate, Ronald Reagan. In addition, she reported on several candidates who were running for the U.S. Senate.

After the election, the young reporter faced disappointment once again when CNN did not offer her a reporting job. Instead, the executives at CNN wanted her to be a writer. To Katie, that seemed like a demotion. Her friends and the coanchors of *Take Two* advised her to take her career elsewhere. It did not seem like the bosses at CNN were going to give the young journalist a break.

So near the end of 1984, Katie moved from Atlanta to Miami, where she took a job with television station WTVJ as a reporter. In her new position, she spent much more time on the air than she ever had at CNN. Frequently she reported on two news stories a day, covering immigration, crime, and drugs. Miami was a hotspot for all of those issues. She listened to the police scanner every day and went out to cover emergencies

Katie covered the 1984 presidential campaign in which Democratic candidate Walter Mondale (right) opposed Republican candidate Ronald Reagan (left). Here the two men shake hands at the beginning of their second debate during the campaign.

that popped up around the city. She worked long, hard hours. Even on Sundays the young reporter often could be found at the television station.

Although Katie's voice had improved, she was still uncomfortable appearing live on the air. She tried hard to get used to the earpiece and other equipment required for live reporting, and she continued to learn the many details of the broadcast business. Years later Katie told a *USA Weekend* reporter how she was often nervous while doing live interviews, and at times even felt like she was going to faint during them. She was much more comfortable if she could tape a piece in advance because then she had the opportunity to cut out the bad parts. Katie liked the reassurance that videotaping provided.

However, Katie's discomfort with doing live interviews didn't stop her from taking such opportunities whenever she could. While she didn't see herself as a news anchor, thinking she was not glamorous enough, she was determined to become a good reporter.

In the meantime, Katie's youthful appearance continued to plague her during her occasional opportunities to anchor the news. Even though she was 28 years old, she still looked much younger. She had gotten a shorter haircut, hoping it would make her look more sophisticated, but the new hairstyle didn't really help. Another time, she took her two best friends with her to buy a new outfit for a show she was scheduled to anchor. Despite the new outfit, station managers remained unimpressed with her on-air presence.

Years later, in an interview with *George* magazine, Katie cringed remembering the reporting opportunities that she missed because others thought she looked too young. Once while on an errand, she heard about a shoot-out in the city. Two FBI agents had been killed. Katie was close to the scene, so she called the station managers and begged to be allowed to cover the story. Instead, executives sent a more experienced reporter even though that person had to drive much farther to get to the crime scene.

This lack of support from her peers wasn't the only reason that Katie began to have doubts about doing live television. She also believed that she did not look like a news anchor. "I always thought of myself as the workhorse, street-reporter type," she once told a writer for the *Chicago Tribune*. "And besides, my bosses never encouraged me."

However, Katie's ambition won out. She continued to work hard, soon becoming known among the

During her years in Miami, Katie gained a great deal of valuable experience at television station WTVJ. However, seeking new challenges, she decided to move back to Washington, D.C., in 1986.

other staffers as a pushy reporter who comfortably voiced her opinion, even if it meant telling everyone else that they were wrong. And her work started winning awards. While at WTVJ, she wrote and produced an award-winning series about child pornography.

But Miami began to bore Katie. Even though she had her own apartment, a job, and a boyfriend in the city, she decided to move on and in 1986 returned to Washington, D.C. There she landed a job at local television station WRC-TV, which was affiliated with the NBC network. The determined young woman was hired as a general assignment reporter for the 11:00 P.M. newscast, again covering crime and other serious issues.

Katie was in her early thirties and reporting for WRC-TV when she covered a story about a dating service for the disabled. For her work, she won a prestigious local Emmy Award. The Associated Press wire service also presented her with an award for that story. NBC executives in New York City began to notice Katie's good work in Washington as well.

But Katie continued to struggle with feeling uncomfortable whenever she was live on the air. When her contract at WRC-TV came up for renewal, her news director advised her to take an anchoring position in a smaller city to get more on-air experience. At the same time, however, she was offered a job by NBC as the number-two reporter covering the Pentagon.

NBC Washington bureau chief Tim Russert had screened about 60 potential candidates for the Pentagon position before selecting Katie. In July 1989 she made her debut on the tough Pentagon beat, where many reporters have difficulty getting people to talk, and information is often hard to come by.

Katie chose the Pentagon assignment instead of an anchoring job because at the time she still wanted to be a reporter. Perhaps growing up near Washington, D.C., with a father in the news business had drawn her to covering government and politics. Whatever the reason for staying in the nation's capital, her work continued to please her bosses.

Katie made covering the Pentagon look easy. Her down-to-earth personality and exuberance won her many friends and contacts. It wasn't long before she was getting information that some of her older, more experienced male colleagues could not get. Reporter

David Martin, who covered the Pentagon for rival network CBS, once said that Katie got a big news scoop the very first week she was on the job—a scoop that he missed. Katie's Pentagon colleagues watched her popularity grow. Some of them reported that at times a line of military officers waited to see her when she arrived at the Pentagon in the morning.

Fred Francis, NBC's chief Pentagon correspondent during those years, claimed to be the person who discovered Katie. He had seen her work in Miami and had recommended her for the Pentagon job. He knew her personality was a plus. "She was really the darling of the building," Francis once told a writer for the *Saturday Evening Post*. "Frequently messages were taped on the door from colonels and generals. One day, someone gave her flowers." As a reporter, Katie could not accept gifts from the sources who provided her with news, but the Pentagon staff continued to cater to her anyway.

Katie had been on the Pentagon beat for only about six months when the U.S. military invaded Panama on December 20, 1989. Its mission was to oust General Manuel Noriega as ruler of the country and replace him with a democratic president. As NBC's chief Pentagon correspondent, Francis went to Panama to cover the event. Couric took over the live telecasts from the Pentagon. Impressed with her work, executives at NBC asked her to cover the Saturday evening news a week later. Finally, Katie was getting a break. It would not be her last one.

When she had first moved back to Washington in 1986, Katie had begun sharing an apartment with Wendy Walker, a friend from her days at CNN. According to Walker, Katie's room was always a mess. Katie did not like to do housework very much, so she did not bother with it. After all, her job kept her very busy.

Two years later, after returning to Washington,

In 1989 when Katie began working for NBC at the Pentagon, she quickly made friends with important military sources and landed a scoop during her first week on the job.

Katie met a man by the name of John Paul Monahan III while attending a party. He was called Jay, for short, and was an attorney. When the two of them met, their attraction was instant. Before being introduced to Katie, Jay had watched her for a while and soon saw she didn't think much of attorneys. He saw her put her finger in her mouth in an imitation of gagging when a few men introduced themselves as lawyers.

So when Jay was introduced to Katie, he told her he was a painter. Quickly charmed by Jay's sense of humor and good looks, Katie agreed to go on a date with him, but not without first asking friends at the newsroom to beep her on her pager so that she could fake an excuse to end the date if things were not clicking. Her precautions proved unnecessary as the two got along well, and Katie continued seeing Jay.

Jay was just two years older than Katie. A native of Long Island, New York, he had graduated in 1977 from Washington and Lee University in Virginia. He was an honors student who played football and lacrosse. After graduating from Washington and Lee, he went to Georgetown University in Washington, D.C., where he attended law school.

Katie found that Jay shared her interest in writing and the news. While in law school, he served as editor of the *Georgetown Law Journal*. After graduating with honors in 1985, he went to work as a clerk for a judge in the U.S. District Court. When Katie met Jay, he was an attorney with the Williams and Connolly law firm in Washington, D.C.

Outside of work, Jay had a strong interest in the U.S. Civil War, a hobby that Katie did not share. He collected Civil War artifacts and occasionally participated in battle reenactments in Virginia's countryside, dressed in full Civil War uniform. Eventually, Katie grew to appreciate Jay's hobby and would often describe him as a Civil War expert.

After dating for about a year, the young couple married in 1989. In recognition of her former roommate's poor housekeeping habits, Katie's friend Wendy Walker gave the bride $90 worth of cleaning supplies as a gift at her wedding shower.

After the wedding, Katie was so busy covering the Pentagon that she could hardly take any time off from her job. Instead of relaxing on her honeymoon, Katie studied the book *Jane's Fighting Ships,* a military directory that describes ships and other military equipment.

When the newlyweds returned from their trip, they settled down in a one-bedroom apartment in downtown Washington. Although a well-organized man, Jay did not seem to mind Katie's chaotic lifestyle. In fact, he marveled at Katie's ability to do so much. Even at home, she amazed Jay, he told a writer for the *Chicago Tribune.* "She'll be lying on the couch, giving attention

In many ways opposites, Katie and her husband, Jay Monahan, appreciated each other's differences. They also shared a love of writing and of the news.

to our Persian cat, Frank, talking on the phone, watching the news on TV, reading *Newsweek* and *Time* and resting all at once." On the other hand, sometimes living with Katie wasn't the most appetizing venture. Jay said he once found a bowl of half-eaten cereal—mixed with cat hairs—under her pillow on their bed!

Eventually Katie and Jay bought a 200-year-old Virginia farmhouse where Jay could keep much of his Civil War artifacts collection. Nestled in the rolling hills of the Shenandoah Valley, the farm made the perfect place for spending quiet weekends away from the hubbub of the city.

It wasn't long before NBC executives gave Katie another break. In May 1990, she was asked to be a national correspondent for the *Today* show. Katie was happy that the job was based in Washington so that she and Jay could continue living there. But only a few months later, an evolving military dispute caused another upheaval in her life. On August 7, U.S. forces were sent to the Persian Gulf in response to Iraq's invasion of the small country of Kuwait five days earlier. Within hours, Katie was back at the Pentagon, covering events that led to another military conflict—the Persian Gulf War.

Katie's Pentagon contacts proved quite useful at this time. On January 16, 1991, an official tipped her off, telling her not to go home at 3:00 P.M. when her shift ended. "And that's how we knew that the air war was going to begin that night," Fred Francis later told a writer for the *Saturday Evening Post*.

Throughout the two-month-long Gulf War, Katie served as the Pentagon correspondent for the *Today* show. Each morning she was at the Pentagon at 5:30, ready to report the news on the show when it went on the air at 7:00 A.M. Viewers around the world became more and more familiar with the friendly face and matter-of-fact approach of Katie Couric.

During the Gulf War Katie had the opportunity to visit Saudi Arabia for three weeks. Her job was to talk with the people of the country who were undergoing the turmoil of war. It was Katie's first overseas assignment and, as she interviewed the Saudi women, one that quickly touched her heart.

Katie also spent time with American troops stationed in the desert. "They helped me appreciate—for the first time in my life—that war is really about people . . . whose lives are at risk," she told *Redbook* magazine several months later. She noted that when she crawled into a sleeping bag under the starlit sky, she was awed by the fact that she was lying in a desert in a country that was in the middle of war. After the war ended on February 28, 1991, she was the first person to interview General Norman Schwarzkopf, who had led the U.S. forces during the war.

When NBC executives teamed Katie Couric with Bryant Gumbel (right) on the Today *show, they gave Katie a big break, but they also created a winning combination.*

4

KATIE'S BIG BREAK

K atie's next career break came on April 4, 1991, when less than a year after she was hired as the *Today* show national correspondent, NBC network executives chose her to be the show's anchor. Katie was thrilled. At 34 years old, she had finally earned the job she had worked for all of her life.

Unlike a reporter who interviews people outside the studio, an anchor usually sits at a desk in the studio and is present on the set throughout an entire broadcast. On the *Today* show the anchors sit in chairs in a conversation area, where their guests sometimes join them. Being an anchor meant that Katie, along with cohost Bryant Gumbel, would be on television for two hours every morning, from 7:00 A.M. to 9:00 A.M. However, the job required a great deal of preparation time, both before and after the broadcast.

Katie had been an unofficial *Today* coanchor since February of that year when a previous anchor, Deborah Norville, took maternity leave. During that time network executives had liked the way Katie enchanted her viewers with her gift of gab. When Deborah did not return to work at the show after her son was born, Katie was glad to officially step in.

Katie didn't find the job easy at first. Chatting with guests and the other *Today* show personalities throughout the early morning hours was not like reporting serious news stories. "It was all very new to me and tough at first and I would get very uptight," Katie told a reporter from *Entertainment Weekly* soon after she started the job.

Today cohost Bryant Gumbel was known for conducting fine interviews and tackling hard questions. Before each show, he spent a great deal of time preparing, reading books and magazine articles about the guests he would be interviewing. He took many notes and formed questions based on the information he learned. Gumbel did the same amount of work when preparing for any topics that would be discussed during the show, whether the subject was serious or lighthearted.

Katie knew she had to be just as dedicated as Bryant. That required hard work. When she was offered the position as cohost of the *Today* show, she had requested that she be assigned as many serious interviews as Bryant. Katie did not want to be an anchor who specialized only in early morning light talk. "That was one of the important conditions of my taking this job—I wasn't going to do all the Martha Stewart segments or lead-ins," Katie told an *Entertainment Weekly* reporter. "I've been in television journalism for 11 years and I didn't want to be this sidekick who sort of giggled and did the features."

Executives at NBC liked Katie, but they were worried about her potential success. At the time, newspaper and magazine stories were circulating that the *Today* show was playing musical chairs with the coanchor's seat. The television audience did not seem to like it when the network replaced Bryant's coanchor for eight years, Jane Pauley, with Deborah Norville in 1990.

They blamed Norville for Pauley's absence, ignoring the fact it was not the newcomer's fault that Jane had left the program. The *Today* show lost many viewers. Norville was on the air for only a few months before she took maternity leave in February.

When Katie took the job the following April, some people thought that she might be there for just a few months and then disappear just as Deborah had. However, Bryant's introduction of Katie during her first day on the job after she became Deborah's replacement showed a lot of confidence in her. "Katie is now a permanent fixture here, a member of our family, an especially welcome one," he announced.

Bryant, who had been an anchor on the *Today* show for nine years, was Katie's opposite. He wore expensive

For years Jane Pauley (left), Bryant Gumbel (right), and Willard Scott (seated) led the Today *show team. But unrest on the show during the months after Jane Pauley left in 1990 fed rumors that Katie would not last long as a cohost.*

suits on the show and kept everything very organized, even color coding his notes according to each guest so he would not get confused while on the air.

On the other hand, Katie was not very organized at all. At home and at the office she left her belongings strewn all over the place. Katie wasn't a fancy dresser either. She liked to shop for her clothes at sales, and she drove a car that was seven years old.

Some people thought Bryant's opinion of his cohost would influence whether network executives kept Katie on the job or not. An anonymous source once told *Time* magazine that Bryant "twinkled" when he was around Katie. But, the anonymous person warned, Bryant's positive opinion of Katie could change quickly. One morning she might "breathe the wrong way" and put her job in danger. Katie thought the situation rather funny. "I can't live my life worrying about Bryant's twinkling," she told one newspaper reporter. "All I can do is the best job I can; I'm not in this job to kowtow to anyone. I'm not out there to make some people like me."

But the television viewers seemed to like Katie a lot. Was it her no-nonsense way of doing interviews? Her quick smile? Her ease at making small talk on the set? No one knew exactly why.

The word used to describe *Today*'s new anchor was "perky," although that was not one of Katie's favorite words. She would have been much happier to have been described as an expert journalist who conducted good interviews. Another word often used to describe her was "cute." She didn't like that term either. For the 12 years since she had graduated from the University of Virginia she had worked to become a professional broadcast journalist. "Cute" did not fit that description.

When Katie accepted the anchor's position she had to make some difficult personal decisions. Not long before the offer at *Today* came, Katie and Jay had moved to a two-bedroom apartment in the Washington suburb of McLean, Virginia, and she was expecting their first child, due to be born in July.

The couple faced another challenge, too. Jay's job in Washington would require him to stay there, at least for a while. So when Katie accepted the job at *Today*, they made the decision to live apart from Monday through Friday. Katie found an apartment in New York City and moved there alone. She and Jay saw each other every weekend, and sometimes he went to New York during the week so they could spend more time together.

At first, few people knew that Katie was pregnant. She was determined to prove that she was capable of being the *Today* anchor, even though she sometimes suffered from morning sickness. But not long after she had accepted the position, Katie announced her pregnancy. NBC executives started planning for the two months that she would be absent after the baby was born.

In the meantime, Katie continued to grow more comfortable in her new role as the *Today* show coanchor, and her popularity grew as well. Television viewers loved her, and the show's ratings continued to rise. Fans who watched the show each morning started sending Katie cards and letters. One woman even sent in hand-knit roller skate booties for the baby.

Some of the letters were complimentary, while others were more critical. Katie thought it was funny that so many people wrote about her hairstyle. One day she received a letter from an 83-year-old man from Scotland. She thought the letter was so funny that she showed it to a reporter from the *Washington Post*. "Dear Katie," the letter read. "Your hair-do is for the birds. You have it puffed up on the left-side, then combed at a straight 45-degree angle. It could readily be the ski slope for an adventurous sparrow. It is totally lacking in symmetry."

Katie laughed at the letter, amazed at how much her hairstyle seemed to mean to some of her viewers.

When the producers of the *Today* show suggested she let her hair grow longer, she refused. Katie wanted it short. It was much easier to care for in the early morning hours. And many women agreed, wanting to copy the look. "Half of America wants her haircut," Anna Febres, the NBC hairstylist, once told a reporter from the *New York Times*. The television viewers seemed to appreciate a television anchor who didn't look perfect every morning. And like many of her fans, Katie didn't wear designer suits and dresses. She chose her own clothes from retail stores like the Gap.

But working on the *Today* show was not only about hair and clothes. Katie took her job very seriously, and over time she gained even more of Bryant's respect. The two got along rather well, joking and laughing during the lighter segments of their morning telecasts. "She's been terrific," Bryant told a *Washington Post* reporter a few weeks after the new cohost's arrival. "Katie's easygoing, she's bright, she's curious, she's fun to be with. I've yet to hear someone say a bad thing about her."

Katie's new job was just one of the many changes happening in her life. In August, just four months after Katie became an anchor, she and Jay had their first baby, Elinor Tully Monahan. Elinor was named after Katie's mother, but Katie and Jay called her Ellie for short. Katie's special name for her tiny new baby was "pea" or "sweet pea."

The new mother took two months off after Ellie was born, then hired a nanny to stay with the baby while she worked. On her first day back on the show, the staff ran a sequence of pictures showing little Ellie. Bryant Gumbel asked Katie if her baby slept through the show. "Only during your interviews," Katie responded, jibing Bryant, who was known for being too stiff on the air. Meanwhile Jay came to New York as often as he could and sometimes took on legal cases in New York for his

Katie's widespread popularity caught her by surprise, but she took her celebrity in stride. Here she poses with fans.

firm so that he could be with his family more often.

It had been a very exciting year for Katie—both as the *Today* show coanchor and as a new mother. She had quickly become a celebrity, with people recognizing her wherever she went. One day, about a year after she started her new job, Katie was shopping in a Gap store in New York City when a woman came up to her and gave her a big hug and a kiss and told her that she loved her.

Such widespread popularity caught Katie by surprise. When some gossip columnists in New York reported that she had been to her first high-fashion show, Katie realized that people recognized her wherever she went.

Even though her life was changing fast, Katie's old friends remained important to her. And despite her newfound popularity, she still felt like a regular person. "My social circle hasn't changed. The idea of dumping my friends for fancier friends is soooo gross!" she told a *People Weekly* reporter in December 1992. "Who would want to do that? I'm not into flamboyant socializing. I'd rather be with my husband. Besides, I'm too tired."

Katie's work for *Today* included both hard and soft news segments; serious interviews were interspersed with lighter moments. For instance, early one morning while Katie and Bryant were on the air live, Gumbel shoved a plate of crackers and headcheese under Katie's nose. (Headcheese is a loaf, resembling lunch meat, but made of gelatin and parts of a pig's organs.) "Try it, come on, it's good, try it!" he urged her.

Reluctantly, Katie took a cracker spread with the head cheese. She champed down on a bite, squinting her eyes together and chewing very slowly. She had a difficult time swallowing it. The staff in the control room whooped and hollered in laughter. Jeff Zucker, the producer of the show, commanded the cameras to zoom in on Katie's face until she finally swallowed the bite. After she was finished, Katie smiled her big, confident smile. Nothing seemed to get her down.

After the headcheese incident, Jeff Zucker could see that Katie was going to be a huge success on *Today*. "Katie's the most natural person I've ever seen in this role," the show's producer told a newspaper reporter from Richmond, Virginia, who was on the scene that day. "She's terrific. This is so new to her and she's getting better every day. She doesn't even realize how good she is."

Katie believed that the viewers loved her because she acted so normal while she was on the air. "I think people see me as someone they could have gone to high school with, or someone who works at the desk next to them," she told a *New York Times* reporter

shortly after she celebrated her one-year anniversary on the show. "I'm ridiculously normal."

Her popularity was undeniable. Whether it was her down-to-earth smile or her early morning cheerfulness, more and more people were watching the show every day, and that made NBC's executives even happier. It was not long before the *Today* show

Although never best friends, Katie and Bryant Gumbel, here outside the Today *show studios, respected each other's professionalism.*

passed its biggest competitor, ABC's *Good Morning America*, in the Nielsen ratings. (The Nielsen ratings provide estimates of the size of the audience that is watching different television shows.)

Talk-show host Larry King invited Katie to be a guest on his show. When one of the call-in viewers asked Katie what advice she would give to an aspiring reporter, she responded with lots of encouragement:

> I think that probably the best advice I could give is that you should get some "on the job" experience. You know, internships were not that prevalent when I was in college; but I worked at radio stations in Washington every summer while I was at the University of Virginia. By the time I graduated, news directors and other people thought, "Wow, she's got some serious work experience; and she's just out of college." So I think internships are a really good idea. . . . You have to be willing to start at the bottom and sweep the floors, and make coffee, and take advantage of where you are. Be willing to come in extra hours; even come in on weekends. Follow reporters around so you can watch the really good ones at work; and learn from them. Just pick everybody's brain you can.

Katie kept up the good work and maintained plenty of energy—even on the days when little Ellie kept her awake half the night. The *Today* show job was exciting, and Katie loved all the opportunities that went along with it. In the summer of 1992, she traveled to Barcelona, Spain, where she covered the Olympics for four weeks. It was a fascinating trip for her viewers as well, as each morning they watched her report on the athletes and events.

A few months later, in October, Katie toured the White House with First Lady Barbara Bush in a live broadcast. The tour included a walk through the State Dining Room, where the president and first lady entertained dignitaries from around the world. Katie and the first lady talked about the painting of Abraham Lincoln that hangs on the wall in that room, as well as

In 1992 when President George Bush (right) joined his wife, Barbara (left), during a live broadcast with Katie at the White House, Katie quickly turned the event into a 20-minute impromptu interview with the president.

the prayer that President John Adams had written to his wife on his second night in the White House. More than 130 years later, President Franklin D. Roosevelt directed workers to carve the same prayer into the mantel of the fireplace. It reads, "I pray heaven to bestow the best of blessings on this house and all who hereafter shall inhabit it. May none but honest and wise men ever rule under this roof." Katie laughed when Mrs. Bush read the word "rule," because it made it sound as if the president were a king who ruled all the land.

As the two women went from room to room, Katie learned a great deal about the history of the home of the U.S. presidents, and Mrs. Bush told her some very funny stories, including one story about former Russian president Boris Yeltsin. Mrs. Bush had accidentally stepped on his foot during dinner one evening when he visited the White House. The following evening at dinner he signed a menu to her. "Dear Barbara, remember it was you who stepped on my foot. You knew what it meant." Yeltsin had explained the tradition to Mrs. Bush earlier. In Russia when a woman stepped on a man's foot, it meant that she loved the man.

After the tour Katie asked Mrs. Bush some questions about her husband's campaign to be reelected as the president. President George Bush was running against Democratic candidate Bill Clinton at the time. In the middle of the live segment, President Bush, surrounded by Secret Service agents, walked into the room. Katie immediately changed into a tough news reporter, asking the president difficult questions about the highly publicized international scandal called the Iran Contra Affair. (Congress was investigating the alleged U.S. involvement with Iran in a scheme that involved providing weapons to rebels in Nicaragua.)

Even though President Bush said he was just passing through, Katie pulled him into a 20-minute impromptu interview. It was very unusual for any reporter to have that kind of opportunity, and Katie grabbed it right away, conducting one of her best interviews ever. Mrs. Bush thought the whole scene rather comical as she watched her husband try to escape from Katie's persistent interrogation.

The 1992 presidential race offered many serious news opportunities, making October 1992 a very important month for Katie and the *Today* show. With the elections coming up in November, Katie had to prepare and conduct many interviews. A week after her White House interview, Katie spoke with Vice President Dan Quayle, who was campaigning for President Bush. In November, after Bill Clinton won the election, Katie was the first person to interview the new first lady, Hillary Rodham Clinton, in the White House.

Katie received a big pay raise after her first year

After the 1992 election, Katie became the first person to interview the new first lady, Hillary Rodham Clinton (left), at the White House.

with *Today*. At the time, newspapers reported that she was making more than $1 million a year. But the *Today* show was not Katie's only interest. At home, she was still a new mother trying to balance her career with an active, 18-month-old daughter. Even though her nanny helped her with the baby, Katie wanted to spend as much time as she could with Ellie. Jay still primarily worked in Washington, D.C., and Katie missed him when he was not in New York. She loved her new job, but life was not easy.

In the early 1990s, Katie was enjoying a full life with a successful career and a growing family.

5

TODAY AND MORE

In the early days of anchoring the *Today* show, Katie was usually in a limousine on her way to work by 5:00 A.M. She had not yet applied makeup, and her hair was a mess. But when she jumped out of the limousine at NBC studios, fans would be waiting for her to sign autographs.

Katie had to arrive at the *Today* studio very early to make preparations for the show that started exactly at 7:00 A.M. While the hair and makeup people worked on her, she drank coffee, which by the time *Today* hit the airwaves helped her appear wide awake. As the rest of the country drank their coffee, Katie and Bryant talked about current events and conducted hard-hitting news interviews with a wide range of people.

The show went off the air at 9:00 A.M., but their work was not finished. Katie and Bryant had to prepare for the next day's show, reviewing information about upcoming guests and sometimes taping interviews in advance. Because she started working so early in the morning, Katie would munch on something like pizza right after the show to tide her over until she went home at 1:30 P.M.

At the duplex in Manhattan, little Ellie and the nanny would usually be waiting. Although the apartment was tiny, its living room rose two stories high, and its large windows looked out onto a courtyard. It was the perfect place for Katie and Ellie—and for Jay when he was in town.

Work would continue at home as well. Sometime during the afternoon Katie would receive a special delivery of notes to go over for the next morning's show.

Some people wondered about Bryant and Katie's working relationship. According to most reports the cohosts were never best friends, but they seemed to respect each other's journalistic style. Katie always thought that Bryant was a crucial part of the *Today* show; she could not imagine the show without him. "I think we complement each other," she told a writer for *TV Guide* in early 1993. "I'm not at my best when Bryant isn't next to me, and I don't think he's at his best when I'm not there to give him a hard time or make fun of him or make sure he's not taking himself oh-too-seriously."

The television audience even seemed to think it was funny when Katie playfully punched Bryant in the arm when they were on the show, as if to say, "C'mon, Bryant, lighten up. We're here for the fun of it." Network executives always heard appreciative comments about such scenes from the viewers, and Katie once said that the playful punches made her popularity rating soar.

Katie was always aware that she did not want to become the morning fluff queen who only reported on soft news stories while Bryant took on the more serious segments. She remained committed to women's issues, interviewing experts on sexual harassment and on health concerns, such as heart disease risks facing women. Still, the show continued to balance both serious and light topics. For example, during one show, Katie first interviewed the director

of the National Institutes of Health, and then in her down-to-earth manner exchanged quips with comedian Jerry Seinfeld.

In addition to Katie's regular work, she would occasionally do television specials. One such program centered on the volunteers who help school children. Katie was touched by the stories she included in the special—such as the segment on an insurance company that encouraged 1,000 of its employees to counsel students in schools weekly. Katie recognized how important it was for children to get enough attention and its effect on their schooling. Another television special Katie hosted focused on adolescent girls and the problems they face in building self-esteem.

Katie also enjoyed the opportunity to take on fun

Katie is committed to dealing with serious issues on the Today *show. In 1994 she interviewed actor Christopher Reeve (right), and his wife, Dana (left) as part of a week-long series on spinal cord injury research.*

side projects, including a guest appearance on *Murphy Brown*, a television program about a fictional woman news anchor. Katie played herself in an episode where she attends a baby shower for the title character.

On the *Today* show, the witty and smart Katie had her share of soft news features. Occasionally she interviewed home-entertainment expert and publisher Martha Stewart. One time, just before Easter, Martha Stewart appeared on the show to demonstrate how to prepare a ham for baking in the oven. When the show was over, Katie wrapped up the ham and took it home, pleased to serve it as her own holiday meal a few days later.

A few years after Katie became the *Today* show anchor, NBC added another position to her already busy schedule. She and news anchor Tom Brokaw were paired up to do a new television news magazine, *Now with Tom Brokaw and Katie Couric*, which broadcast from 9:00 P.M. to 10:00 P.M. each Wednesday. Jeff Zucker, the *Today* show producer, also produced *Now*. Katie saw the show as another opportunity to conduct meaty interviews with strong news angles.

For the first *Now* show, Katie did a story about Baby Jessica, a toddler whose adoptive parents and biological parents were fighting for custody of the child. Other *Now* shows featured stories about crimes and celebrities, as well as pieces about shootings, pipe bombs, and murders. Katie once did a segment on a 45-year-old Los Angeles woman who became a police officer and then was killed just a few days later. Interspersed among the serious stories were segments about celebrities such as actress Bette Midler, talk-show host Conan O'Brien, actor Robert De Niro, comedian Robin Williams, basketball star Michael Jordan, and author Caroline Kennedy.

Despite its good reporting, *Now* never managed to gain strong ratings or to challenge its competitors in the crowded television newsmagazine market. CBS's

When NBC executives paired Katie with news anchor Tom Brokaw to host the news-magazine Now, *they had great hopes. However, the show never matched its competitors in the ratings.*

60 Minutes remained one of the most popular news-magazines. By November 1994, NBC had reformatted *Now* to become one of its series of *Dateline* shows. Katie returned to her early morning routine for the *Today* show, where her popularity continued to grow.

Being an anchor on a highly rated television show brings its own fame. Writers at magazines and news-papers were always calling Katie, trying to set up interviews with her. She even granted a story to an editor at *Ladies Home Journal* about her new apartment on the West Side of New York City. The May 1994 move had marked a big moment for the family. For the first time since Katie joined the *Today* show as the anchor, she, Jay, and Ellie would be living together in one place. Jay had started working for a Manhattan law firm.

The apartment was more spacious than the last one, which was a good thing since Ellie was an active two-year-old toddler. Katie was thrilled to set up a permanent residence for her family. She chose a blue-and-white color scheme for the living room, with its wide window looking out over the city. Jay's mother gave them a table for the dining room. The room's overall decor made it a warm, inviting place for the couple to entertain.

Katie was glad that her family was finally together. Although still deeply involved with her career, Katie treasured spending time with her daughter. Ellie, of course, liked to watch television. Sometimes she watched the shows featuring her mother, but she enjoyed PBS's *Reading Rainbow* more than anything else.

As Ellie grew older, Katie was amused to see her daughter pick up some of her habits. Katie remembered her own mother giving directions to her and her siblings and then saying, "And I mean it!" At first, Katie may not have noticed that she used the phrase herself when she was talking to little Ellie, but one day it struck her. "The other day, I overheard Ellie in the playground, bossing around the other little kids, [telling them,] 'And I mean it!'" Katie told *Glamour* magazine.

When she was not with Ellie, Katie still made her work top priority. From the windows in her office, she could easily see Rockefeller Plaza, but Katie had little time to daydream out the window. The early morning television programs—including *Good*

Morning America on ABC—were fierce competitors. They often fought to get the same interviews. The morning shows also competed with many prime-time news magazine shows, such as *20/20* and *60 Minutes,* and it seemed like every news show wanted to interview the same people.

In the 1990s Katie was going up against many other women in the broadcast business who were also very good at their jobs. Barbara Walters had blazed a trail for women in the news business. Walters and Diane Sawyer, another well-known journalist, appeared on the ABC news shows *20/20* and *PrimeTime.* CBS featured the popular Connie Chung. Even at NBC, Katie faced friendly rivalries. Jane Pauley, who had been a *Today* anchor and now anchored *Dateline,* was another one of the many news people competing for the big interviews.

But Katie did not view herself as being in the same ranks as Barbara Walters and Diane Sawyer. "Barbara's the queen," she told a writer for *Vanity Fair* in an interview at a café near NBC studio headquarters in New York City. "I think once you build up a track record and you've interviewed so many world leaders, and so many people have entrusted their stories to you, that definitely works to [Barbara's] advantage. She never takes a breather. She's always in there."

Generally, Katie's assistants and the producers at the *Today* show would call to schedule interviews with people. Sometimes, though, when the staff was not having much luck lining up an important interview, Katie would pick up the telephone and make the call herself. In an interview with *Vanity Fair* she described a typical call: "Hi, Katie Couric calling from the *Today* show. . . . I'd be very interested in having you come on our [program] to discuss your problem/story/solution/tragedy/invention/heartbreak/fill in the blank. I'm very interested in your story—which 9 times out of 10 I am—and I think you would be very comfortable talking to me." Of course, sometimes

Veteran ABC news journalists Barbara Walters (left) and Sam Donaldson pose with coworker Connie Chung, formerly with CBS. They rank among the top news anchors who have competed with Katie Couric through the years to secure the big interviews.

the person she was talking to would agree to the interview, but other times they would not.

The pace of life at Katie's home remained busy. When Ellie woke up a lot during the night, Katie went to work exhausted. Such unpredictability in her schedule did not help her get better organized. Ellie's nanny Nancy Poznek, an older woman who doted on the little girl, also helped Katie organize her clothing and her checkbook. Occasionally, Ellie and the nanny visited Katie in her NBC office. Ellie would color pictures while she was there. Sometimes Katie would take a break to have lunch with her daughter and the nanny. However, these daytime escapes with her daughter had to be tucked into Katie's busy routine at *Today*.

In 1994, one of the hot news stories involved Olympic ice skater Tonya Harding, who was found to be behind an attack on skater Nancy Kerrigan while the two women were competing in Michigan for the national amateur skating title. An assailant had struck Kerrigan on the knee, injuring her so badly that she had to withdraw from the competition. Katie kept trying to get an interview with Tonya Harding, whose ex-husband was charged with conspiracy in the attack. Couric would call Harding's attorneys two to three times a day. The *Today* anchor's also showed sharp wit and sense of humor. She once sent Harding's attorney a birthday cake that read, "We refuse to stop sucking up!" In the end none of Katie's attempts worked. Connie Chung got the interview after pursuing Harding for ten days in the ice skater's home of Portland, Oregon.

That year another major news story involved the murder of the ex-wife of former football star O. J. Simpson, Nicole Brown Simpson, and her friend Ronald Goldman. All of the networks wanted to interview Simpson. For Katie and the *Today* show, there was an added twist to the drama: Bryant Gumbel was a good friend and golf pal of O. J. Simpson. As other newscasters pointed toward the football star as the possible murderer, Bryant adamantly assured viewers that his friend could have never committed such a crime. He defended Simpson both on and off the camera. Little did Katie and Bryant know at the time that the upcoming O. J. Simpson trial would be one of the biggest news stories of the century.

Just around the time that O. J. Simpson was arrested and jailed for the murders, the *Today* show moved into a glamorous new studio that had a glass wall three-stories high overlooking the plaza at Rockefeller Center. President Clinton was the first person to be interviewed the day the new studio was unveiled. He answered questions asked by New Yorkers who were walking outside the studio.

Now producer Jeff Zucker eventually returned to producing the *Today* show. Under his guidance, the program continued to increase in the television ratings. Everyone at *Today* knew that they were in a tough competitive battle with first-place *Good Morning America*. They put in the hard work needed to succeed, and before long the dreams of NBC executives seemed to be coming true. *Today* was well on its way to becoming the top-rated early morning television talk show.

But at the same time, studio executives had other concerns. Bryant's three-year, $7-million contract had run out and they had to negotiate a new contract with him. However, other networks, including FOX and CBS, were also interested in hiring Bryant. Eventually, he signed on with NBC for one more year and $3 million.

Not long after Bryant signed his new contract, Katie Couric had another surprise for her television viewers. She and Jay were expecting their second child. The day the news was announced to the television audience, the show's new weatherman, Al Roker, pushed a baby carriage onto the set. Katie quipped: "I know people think I need to lay off the jelly doughnuts because they haven't seen my waist in weeks."

For the second time, viewers watched Katie grow into an expectant mom right before their eyes. Katie found herself in a new role: she had become a fashion symbol for pregnant women around the world. Women called the show to find out where Katie had purchased a piece of clothing or jewelry worn on the air. Katie even talked with a reporter for *InStyle* magazine about her five secrets to maternity fashion:

Tennis legend Chris Evert (left) points to Katie's new maternity wear during the Today *show host's second pregnancy. The two friends posed at the International Tennis Hall of Fame gala on September 8, 1995.*

think vertically, accessorize, avoid bows and puffy sleeves, forget jumpsuits, and go for clean lines in luxurious fabrics.

Many other issues besides Katie's pregnancy interested people at the time. In the fall of 1994, viewers around the world remained glued to their television sets as they watched the O. J. Simpson criminal trial unfold. At the end of the trial, O. J. Simpson was found not guilty of the murder. Afterward he decided to grant his first interview to NBC. Network executives chose Katie, Bryant, and Tom Brokaw to conduct the

O. J. Simpson tries on gloves put in evidence during the famous 1994 trial; Simpson was charged with the murders of his ex-wife, Nicole Brown Simpson, and her friend Ronald Goldman. Katie's cohost on the Today *show, Bryant Gumbel, defended Simpson both on and off camera.*

interview. Then O. J. Simpson's lawyers pointed out that Bryant might have a conflict of interest because of his friendship with Simpson. The network executives agreed, and Bryant was told he could not participate in the interview.

That decision offended Bryant so much that he skipped a whole week of work. Matt Lauer, the newsreader on the program, was called in as his replacement. Ultimately the interview never took place. Simpson's attorneys thought he should not talk to the press since Nicole Brown's and Ronald Goldman's families had filed civil lawsuits against him. Katie learned of the canceled interview only after she and Tom had flown to Los Angeles to meet with O. J. Simpson.

As these events unfolded, Bryant Gumbel reached

a decision. Although he had signed another one-year contract with the network, he announced that when that period was over, he would leave *Today*. His departure would mark the end of 15 years he had spent as one of the show's cohosts.

In the midst of these changes at *Today*, Katie's family welcomed its newest member. Caroline Couric Monahan was born in January 1996, and Katie took two months of maternity leave. Jay often helped with the baby, especially when Katie was on assignments that took her away from home.

As the difficulties of building two high-profile careers while caring for two young children became evident, the couple decided to employ a second nanny. This woman helped with the baby, while Ellie kept her first nanny. Carrie's nanny eventually became the person to get up at night with the baby so that Katie could get the rest she needed. She usually tried to go to bed at 9:30 or 10:00 P.M., because she still had to get up in time to leave for the studio each morning at 5:00.

Katie's work schedule never slowed down. During the summer of 1996, she traveled to the Olympics in Atlanta to cover the event for NBC. Always one for a laugh, she found a manicurist who could recreate the long and flashy fingernails made famous by Olympic runner Gail Devers. But events turned deadly serious early in the morning of the ninth day of the games. On Saturday, July 27, a pipe bomb exploded in Atlanta's Centennial Olympic Park, killing one woman and injuring more than 100 other people.

The *Today* show staff arranged to interview temporary security guard Richard Jewell, who moments before the explosion had detected the unclaimed knapsack in which the bomb was hidden. Jewell had immediately notified authorities, and they began evacuating the park. Experts credited the security guard's quick action with saving many people's lives.

But within days, reporters used circumstantial evidence to portray Richard Jewell as the primary suspect in the bombing. Those charges were later proven false, and NBC paid Jewell an undisclosed sum as part of an out-of-court settlement of a lawsuit he filed against the network.

The bombing overshadowed the final days of the Olympics, but Katie and the rest of the NBC staff still faced the challenge of providing national coverage of the remaining events. This unusually busy schedule did not let up when the Olympics ended.

In addition to reporting on the summer games, Katie also was busy with coverage of the upcoming presidential election. In one interview she got into a heated discussion about the tobacco industry with Republican presidential candidate Bob Dole. Talking to a writer from *George* magazine, Matt Lauer applauded the way Katie did her interviews: "It's impossible for politicians not to be charmed by her. Then, all of a sudden, just when they're feeling real comfortable and they're sinking into their chair, the next thing you know, Pow! Right in the kisser!"

Despite Katie's personal successes, times were tense on *Today*. Everyone knew that Bryant would soon be leaving and Katie would be working with a new cohost. Then another bomb hit the *Today* staff. Producer Jeff Zucker was diagnosed with colon cancer in October 1996. Katie immediately went to work to help Zucker face this crisis. She researched the disease and its treatments and found the best cancer specialist in New York. She was a steadfast friend to Zucker as he underwent surgery to remove the cancer and then endured chemotherapy treatments to make sure that the disease did not spread. Just two months later Zucker was back at work, and Katie and the rest of the *Today* staff breathed a collective sigh of relief.

Bryant, meanwhile, was packing his bags. When he had announced that he was leaving the show, NBC

executives asked Katie if she wanted to be the sole anchor. But Katie preferred to have a cohost, and Matt Lauer got the promotion on January 6, 1997. Eventually, Bryant accepted a contract of $7 million per year with rival network CBS.

On December 2, 1996, Katie, Al Roker, and Matt Lauer showed up on *The Oprah Winfrey Show* in a salute to Bryant. Weeks later Jeff Zucker produced Bryant's last show, a tribute to the 15 years the anchor had spent on the program. Bryant and Katie joked about his reputation as a control freak. Many celebrities, including First Lady Hillary Clinton and former president George Bush, as well as actors John Travolta, Tom Cruise, and Sandra Bullock, sent

Katie and other members of the NBC staff covered the 1996 summer Olympics in Atlanta, Georgia. The final days of the games were overshadowed by the July 27 explosion of a bomb in Atlanta's Centennial Olympic Park. The Olympic flag flies at half mast in honor of the dead and the injured.

On January 3, 1997, his last day as cohost of the Today *show, Bryant Gumbel (seated) takes in a standing ovation from his colleagues. Joining in the applause are (from left) Al Roker, Katie Couric, Matt Lauer, Gene Shalit (partially obscured), and Willard Scott.*

video tributes to be aired during Bryant's last show, January 3, 1997. Gumbel had made many friends while working on *Today*. Other celebrities visited the studio during his final show, including the singer Prince, boxer Muhammad Ali, and comedian Tracey Ullman. Katie wrote a silly and heartfelt poem in honor of her coanchor. After summarizing Bryant's early career, she read:

> When I entered the picture after a few years
> You welcomed me and helped me overcome all my fears.
> You gave me some rope, but did not let me hang.
> So what will this Ying do without her Yang? . . .
> There's no other you. Perspicacious, pugnacious, persistent, and proud
> You may not be a smoocher, but you can sure work a crowd.

Then Katie ended her poem with these words:

Your smarts and your skills cannot be denied.
You home right on it, and you let nothing slide.
You're a hard nut to crack, but inside you're like butter.
You can be a sweetheart and an annoying big brother.
While I've made it clear that you're perfectly sluggable
There are times where you are, dare I say it, quite huggable.

Finally, it was Bryant's turn for the grand finale. "It's been a pleasure and a genuine privilege to represent this program and the wonderful, wonderful people who put it on," he said. "I've had a great time. I really have. I've had a great time. I hope that you've enjoyed it nearly as much—even a fraction as much as I have. And thank you all very much. I mean that."

Then, holding glasses of champagne, the *Today* staff toasted Bryant. Weatherman Al Roker led them in a standing ovation. With Bryant's departure, a new era was dawning for everyone involved with the *Today* show.

A giant poster in the window of NBC studios at Rockefeller Plaza in New York City displays images of Katie and her new cohost Matt Lauer. The Today *show continued to earn good ratings after Matt teamed up with Katie, but both Katie and Matt soon faced personal tragedies.*

6

FOREVER JAY

Viewers liked the *Today* show's new anchor, Matt Lauer, and the show's good ratings showed the NBC executives that he was a comfortable partner for Katie. Matt's on-air style reflected Katie's own style. There was none of the formality that Bryant had brought to the show, and Matt and Katie easily chatted their way through each morning.

Matt had started his television career in 1979 as producer of noon news on WOWK-TV, in Huntington, West Virginia. After anchoring four television news programs that struggled to survive in major cities, he spent a year and a half looking for the right job. Finally in 1992 executives from WNBC, a local station in New York City, called him to anchor the show *Today in New York*. Two years later, NBC executives selected Matt to become the news-reader on the *Today* show. When Bryant resigned, Matt became Katie's coanchor.

Matt had been in the coanchor's spot only a few weeks when he received bad news. His father, who lived in Florida, had become very sick with lung cancer. From his bed, the elderly man was thrilled that he had lived to see that his son had made it big in the broadcasting business. Every Friday when the *Today* broadcast finished, Matt hopped on a plane and flew to Florida for the weekend. He returned to the set just in time for the Monday morning show. Matt's father watched *Today* daily from his bed until he died the next spring.

With Katie and Matt as coanchors the popularity of the *Today* show continued to grow. After several years on the job, Katie was very comfortable on the air. Jeff Zucker was one of her biggest fans. "[She] is the kid on the playground, not the dolled-up, glamorous, ready-for-prime-time anchor. Perhaps we defined morning television for the nineties, by mistake, when we found Katie," he once said.

But with all her fame and fortune, Katie changed very little. Old friends said the only difference was that she dressed better now that she was a celebrity. Even though her Rockefeller Center office was decorated with letters from George Bush, Hillary Clinton, and other famous people, Katie Couric remained very much the same.

At home, family life with one-year-old Carrie and five-year-old Ellie kept Katie and Jay extremely busy. Katie sometimes rushed from the NBC studios to Ellie's nursery school to pick her up before they headed home. One particular day when Katie arrived, she was sure Ellie had been dressed by Jay that morning. Her long curls were tangled, but her little denim jumper sported a stylish Pocahontas on its front. After having pizza with her mother, Ellie was off to a computer class for part of the afternoon.

All day long, Katie seemed to rush from one assignment to the next, whether it was as a professional broadcaster or as a dedicated mother. Still, she loved her life and considered herself very fortunate. Every day she tried to be at home by 3:00 P.M. to spend time with Ellie and Carrie. She usually prepared dinner for her family, drawing on her memories from her own childhood when the Couric kids and their parents gathered around the dining room table at suppertime. Katie stayed in touch with her parents, who lived near Washington, D.C. She talked with them frequently on the telephone.

Each morning on *Today*, Katie, Matt, and Al Roker enjoyed mixing with the crowd that gathered outside the *Today* show set. Even in the cold winds of a New York winter, people gathered to watch through the glass windows as the *Today* set went up. Near the end of the broadcast, Katie and the other *Today* celebrities ventured outside to meet and greet the fans. They shook hands and talked to the people who had watched and waved to the cameras during the two hours of the show. Frequently Katie went back outside again after the show ended to sign autographs and let her fans have their pictures taken with her.

Katie's popularity continued to grow. In 1997 more than 10 million people around the world were watching the *Today* show. For many people who watched the show, it seemed Katie's life had become part of their lives. Along with her celebrity came many awards. In February Proctor and Gamble took a poll for Scope mouthwash for Valentine's Day to determine America's most kissable celebrity. Katie was the winner. Organizations invited her to moderate many events, including an awards ceremony hosted by the New York Public Library.

Meanwhile Jay had settled into a new position as a legal analyst for the MSNBC network. He regularly appeared as a guest commentator on Geraldo Rivera's show *Rivera Live,* which aired on the CNBC channel. But soon Jay began to have problems with his health, with complaints of feeling tired and achy. At first, he blamed his fatigue on his extensive travel—he had been flying back and forth between the East and West

Coasts to cover the O. J. Simpson civil trial for MSNBC. Katie recalled later, "We thought [his health] would get better when his schedule improved." Then, in April 1997, Jay was diagnosed with colon cancer, the same disease that Jeffrey Zucker had successfully battled the year before.

Colon cancer affects the large intestine, the organ that takes waste products from digested food out of the body. It is estimated that more than 130,000 new cases of colon cancer or cancer of the rectum are diagnosed each year in this country. The average age for developing colon cancer is 62 years old. Both Jeff and Jay were young compared to others who had gotten the disease.

Jay underwent surgery just a few weeks after the cancer was discovered, and doctors expected him to recover fully. "The two most important men in my life getting it was just so hard to believe," Katie later told a *Newsweek* reporter. "I would wake up every day and say, 'I can't believe Jay got it.'"

Colon cancer is an unpredictable disease. Katie and Jay put up a strong battle on the home front. Katie pulled out the information about the disease she had gathered back when Jeff Zucker had been diagnosed with colon cancer. But even after surgery, the disease continued to devastate Jay's body.

Katie's busy schedule continued. In January 1998, the news of White House intern Monica Lewinsky's alleged affair with President Clinton jarred the American public. Producers at the *Today* show, like all the other news agencies in the country and many across the world, were very interested in the situation. Although Monica Lewinsky and her former friend, Linda Tripp, were unavailable for television interviews, their attorneys and spokespersons made several appearances on the morning talk shows. President Clinton denied the allegations.

Meanwhile, Jay's illness weighed heavily on Katie's

Colon Cancer

Ninety-nine percent of all Americans do not think of colon cancer as a fatal disease, says a government survey released in March 2000 by Capitol Hill. The startling fact is that colon cancer is the second most common cause of cancer death in the United States, surpassed only by lung cancer. According to the American Cancer Society, more than 130,000 people are diagnosed with the disease each year, and about 56,000 will die from it over the next 12 months.

Colon cancer strikes blacks and whites, both women and men, young and old alike. It often strikes without warning, and even people who are young, healthy, nonsmoking, and have no family history of colon cancer are not guaranteed of avoiding it.

However, colon cancer is a curable disease. According to Carolyn Aldigé, president of the Cancer Research Foundation of America, almost no one needs to die from colon cancer. It is easy to spot with routine tests, and in almost all cases is curable if discovered at an early stage. Experts estimate that death from colon cancer would drop by 50% to 75%, and that between 30,000 and 40,000 lives would be saved each year, if more people would simply be tested routinely.

mind. With help from people at NBC, she spent long hours researching the disease. It was very frustrating that she could not find anything that seemed to help cure his cancer. She just wanted to help Jay get better. "I can't tell you how many doctors and biotech companies and hospitals we talked to," said friend and NBC employee Lori Beecher to a *Newsweek* reporter. "One doctor said he used our book [of research] to help other people find clinical trials. But unfortunately, it wasn't in time to help Jay."

After months of watching her deal with Jay's illness, some of Katie's friends decided she needed a break. They took her on a vacation to the Bahamas to celebrate her 41st birthday.

First Lady Hillary Clinton was scheduled to appear on the *Today* show on January 27 to talk about child care, one of her many projects. After the Lewinsky story broke, Katie was looking forward to asking the first lady about her feelings about the scandal. It would be Mrs. Clinton's first public reply to the accusations against her husband. Many Americans wondered how

Dr. Douglas Rex of the Indiana University Medical Center in Indianapolis shows a colonoscope, used to look for evidence of colon cancer and other medical conditions.

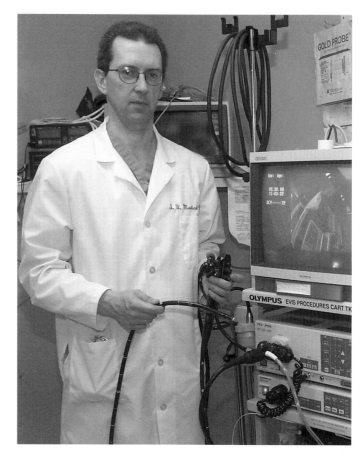

the first lady was feeling. The week that Katie returned from her vacation she spent many hours preparing for the interview with Mrs. Clinton.

While the Clinton-Lewinsky affair occupied the minds of many Americans, few viewers knew that Katie and Jay were fighting their own battle. On Friday, January 23, after the *Today* show ended, Katie went directly to the Manhattan hospital where Jay lay terribly ill.

Jay died the following day, Saturday, January 24, 1998. His death was unexpected news to many people. "John Paul Monahan III, a lawyer and NBC News legal analyst, died Saturday at Lenox Hill Hospital in Manhattan," stated his obituary in the following Monday's *New York Times*. "The husband of Katie

Couric, the host of NBC's 'Today' program, Mr. Monahan was 42 and lived in Manhattan."

Katie was numbed by the pain. Her interview with Hillary Clinton never took place. That Monday on the *Today* show Matt had the difficult task of announcing Jay's death to the viewers. The next day, Matt conducted the interview with Mrs. Clinton. During that interview, the first lady said that she did not believe the president had been involved with Monica Lewinsky. Mrs. Clinton also said that she thought other people were purposefully trying to make her husband look bad.

But by this time, the Lewinsky scandal was one of the furthest things from Katie's mind. She and Jay had been married for nine years, and she could not believe he was gone. Throughout his illness, she had continued to work regularly on the *Today* show, hoping that everything would soon return to normal. But when Jay died, Katie felt very alone. She was suddenly the single mother of two little girls. Her parents were very supportive, even though sometimes Katie did not feel like talking to them. Friends struggled to find the right words. Jay's six siblings and their parents kept in constant touch. In a show of sympathy, viewers of the *Today* show and many others sent contributions to the National Cancer Institute.

Nothing seemed to help Katie feel better. Jay's death forced her to go through a slow mourning process. She cried many tears and took some comfort in her two daughters. She also received some consolation from talking with people who knew Jay well. She even received a copy of Jay's college transcripts and read his entrance essay for college. For her two little girls, Katie put together a book of letters that people wrote to her about their father. She added one of her own about how she met their father and why she loved him so much.

For the first time in her life, Katie knew the pain of

MARCH 13, 2000 $3.50

TIME

WHEN KIDS KILL KIDS

ECSTASY BOOM   G.O.P. HOLY WAR

Katie Couric lost her husband to **COLON CANCER.** Now she's spreading the word: Get tested and save your life!

PLUS: What you can do to prevent it

Katie's Crusade

Committed to preventing other people from facing the pain she and her late husband, Jay, experienced as he fought cancer, Katie started a campaign to increase colon cancer awareness and to raise funds for research of the disease.

losing someone whom she loved. When she had been younger, she had once said that the worst thing that ever happened to her was not being named captain of her high school cheerleading squad. Now everything had changed. Losing Jay was devastating.

Jay's death was, perhaps, the most personal tragedy that Katie ever experienced. Publicly, she never talked about the pain he was in, the symptoms he felt, or how his illness affected either one of them. Katie was very careful to allow Jay to die with dignity.

After taking a month off to spend time at home with her daughters, Katie wanted her family to get a feeling of normalcy back in their lives. With her smile not quite as bright as it had always been, she returned to work on the *Today* show.

Appearing on March 6, 2000, before a Senate Special Committee on Aging, Katie testifies about her husband's fight against colon cancer, focusing on the importance of colorectal cancer screening tests. Jay's death has forced Katie to build a new life.

7

A NEW LIFE

On the day that Katie returned to television, she wore Jay's wedding band on a chain around her neck, as a silent reminder of the man whom she loved so much. On that cold February morning, Katie thanked the viewers of *Today* for all the support they had given her. More than 10,000 cards and letters had flooded the *Today* show's offices while Katie was absent.

"Words, of course, will never describe how devastating this loss has been for me and my daughters and all of Jay's family as well," Katie told her viewers. "But the heartfelt and compassionate letters and cards that so many of you have sent to me were enormously comforting, and I'm so grateful."

Even in the most difficult of times, Katie's down-to-earth warmth came through.

"It's great to have you back," said Matt.

Katie thanked him and reached out to squeeze his hand. Then she settled down to work. That day she interviewed two very important people. She asked U.S. secretary of state James Baker

Katie interviews Donatella Versace (left), the sister of murdered fashion designer Gianni Versace. Katie's personal loss has made her more compassionate toward others who have faced similar hardship.

questions about the international conflict in Iraq. Later she talked with William Ginsburg, the attorney for Monica Lewinsky. She also congratulated Tara Lipinski for winning the Olympic Gold Medal for figure skating.

Going back to work so soon after Jay's death was not easy. But Katie knew it would help her and her daughters return to a routine and heal from their loss. She was very glad that the people at NBC were supportive during such a difficult time.

The show's weatherman, Al Roker, later said that Katie's composure her first day back on the job helped everyone else on the *Today* show, too. "Her demeanor put us all at ease," he told a *Newsweek* reporter. In the hardest of times, Katie's compassion was apparent. Somehow she could still help other people relax.

Back home, Katie's life had changed drastically. She was faced with the fact that she was now the sole parent for her two daughters. Jay was no longer around to help with the little things, like paying the bills and cleaning the house. Besides, Katie understandably missed his friendship. She was very quiet about sharing her feelings, though. She only talked about them with close friends and family members. She never shared the full story with her television audience, and she gave fewer interviews to her counterparts in the media.

Many of Katie's colleagues in the news business wanted to talk to her about Jay's death. Eventually, she agreed to an interview with Rick Marin, a reporter from *Newsweek*. "It's very hard to live out a personal tragedy on national television," Katie told Rick. "Every day my heart was breaking."

Katie felt her grief should be a private matter, but privacy was difficult to attain when millions of people around the world were watching the *Today* show every morning. Many of those people felt as if they were part of Katie's family. Once again, Katie was reminded of the difficulties of being a celebrity. "Sometimes I just forget how public a figure I am," she told the *Newsweek* reporter. "So many people in the crowd [that gathers each day outside the *Today* show window] are really kind and say I'm in their prayers, and I just say thank you and move on, because it's sort of sacred. It's hallowed ground for me. It's not something I want to engage in."

Katie remained reticent about the pain of losing her husband or the difficulty of his illness. One of the first times she mentioned it was when she was honored at the June 1998 Avon Women of Enterprise Awards, held in New York City. Katie gave a 15-minute keynote speech, saying that in the past year she had learned that life was tenuous and short. "How do you go on when fate delivers such a crushing blow that it causes permanent damage to your heart?" she asked the crowd. "I've often wondered. People ask how and why do you go on and do what you have to do. I do it because I have two girls who are depending on me to show them what you have to do when life throws you a major curve ball."

Soon after that speech Katie started to talk more often about colon cancer. Just a few months after returning to the air, she came up with an idea: she could spare other people from the pain that Jay had suffered by using her role as a television broadcaster to get a message across. Katie and the *Today* show staff began putting together the information that they had gained about colon cancer. "I can't bear to see other families going through this," she told a *Newsweek* reporter.

In September Katie presented a five-part series about colon cancer on the *Today* show. She wanted people to know that they needed to get checkups. Katie has a short, blunt saying about the disease: "Get your butt to the doctor! It could save your life." Her series was well received. NBC executives decided to use part of it on *NBC Nightly News,* as well as on MSNBC.

With anti-cancer activist Lilly Tartikoff and the Entertainment Industry Foundation, Katie founded an organization called the National Colorectal Cancer Research Alliance. It encourages further study of colon cancer so that a cure can eventually be found.

Even though the year following Jay's death was difficult, each morning on the *Today* show, Katie looked like she was having a good time. When her contract with NBC came up for renewal that year, Katie found that other networks were interested in hiring her. But she decided to stay with NBC, the network that had given her so much support during Jay's illness and after his death.

Katie also participated in other charity work. That December, she and her coworkers autographed a leather jacket and a T-shirt and put it up for auction on e-Bay, an Internet auction website. The *Today* show staff planned to use the money for Toys for Tots, a charity group that buys toys for needy children. The proceeds from the sale of the jacket went toward that cause.

As a serious broadcast journalist, Katie regularly had to face tragedy on the national and personal level. On April 20, 1999, two students armed with guns and bombs opened fire at Columbine High School in Littleton, Colorado, killing 13 people and wounding more than 30 others before taking their own lives. Katie became one of the first national news broadcasters to arrive at the scene. Two days after the shooting spree, she interviewed family members of those who died in the ordeal. As she talked with the father of Isaiah Shoels, a student who was killed that day, her sympathy and compassion were very apparent.

Police stand outside Columbine High School in Littleton, Colorado, on April 20, 1999, shortly after two teenagers opened fire on fellow students. The next day, Katie interviewed family members of two of the slain students.

"Mr. Shoels, thank you so much for being here," Katie said. "We are so terribly sorry about your son. I understand from everyone at the school that Isaiah was extremely well-loved by the students, a very popular young man. Can you tell me a little about him?"

"Well, Isaiah was very outgoing," Michael Shoels responded. "He . . . had a lot to live for, you know what I'm saying? And I really do feel that he was taken out a little bit too early."

Katie focused closely on Michael Shoels and on what he said about Isaiah. She knew well the pain that this father was feeling over the loss of his son. As the interview continued, Columbine student Craig Scott, whose sister died during the shootings, talked about what happened.

"How are your parents doing, Craig?" Katie asked.

"They're grieving over it. But we're going to get through this. I really . . . it's a life-changing experience for me, and I really—I really put—I really trust God's hands over this. And I believe He's going to be there for us."

Eventually, Katie turned her attention back to Isaiah's father. "Mr. Shoels, for you the last 24 hours plus, I know, have been unbearable for you and your family."

"It's been really agonizing," Mr. Shoels responded. Later he added, "I'm really hurting inside, because, you know I want to be in denial, but I know he wouldn't want this. . . . I love my children more than life itself. And I hope the parents out there can feel where I'm coming from because, you know, our kids [are] our future. That's all we have. . . . We need to watch and take care of them."

Katie went on to ask how the rest of the Shoels family was doing. Then, very seriously, she closed the interview. "Michael Shoels, Craig Scott. I don't know how to thank you all for coming to share these terrible feelings with us. I know how difficult it is. Thank you both so much. That was beautiful."

After a commercial break, Katie and Matt continued talking about the Columbine disaster. "Katie, I don't think I've ever seen a more compelling and emotional interview than the one you just conducted between Mr. Shoels and Craig Scott," Matt told her.

"It's unbelievable," Katie said to Matt and the millions of viewers who were watching the show. "And I think these two men, this father and this young man, really sum up the agony of this entire community. A father who lost his son is such a senseless tragedy, and a young man who had to face things that really people only face in combat situations. But I was so moved as I saw Mr. Shoels reach over for Craig Scott's hand, and they were somehow affirming that together with the help of the community that somehow these people some way will heal."

The day was quite emotional for viewers of the *Today* show, as well as for its hosts. Katie knew well the pain that families in Littleton, Colorado, were experiencing. The feelings from her own loss over Jay's death were still fresh. She realized that it took great courage for those family members to appear on television, and her admiration and respect for those families came through.

Her own experience with grief has made Katie more compassionate toward other people who have lost a loved one. She never brings up her tragic loss, but frequently she grips the hands of people she interviews who are going through personal problems and expresses her sorrow for them.

Jay's death forced Katie to think about her life and the lives of her daughters. First she decided to sell the Virginia farmhouse that she and Jay had purchased soon after they were married. They had spent many happy times there as a family. But she needed to be more practical. She and Ellie and Carrie would be spending more time in New York City, so a Virginia home really didn't fit in their lives anymore.

After making that decision, Katie bought an apartment in New York City and quickly went to work getting it ready for the girls. She loved the new apartment the minute she walked through the door. Decorating the new home with her daughters kept her busy for several months.

Katie chose bright colors and fun furnishings for the girls. Ellie's room was done with bold, blue-striped wallpaper, and the bedspread featured tiny print floral patterns in blue and white. Carrie's bedroom featured tiny prints in pinks, blues, and yellows.

One day Katie showed Joanna Powell, a writer for *Good Housekeeping*, around her redecorated apartment. The reporter noted that the refurbished home seemed a sign of a new beginning. The apartment reflected Katie's life, a life without Jay but a life full of fun with her girls. "I feel like I've grown up," Katie observed. "This is a grown-up apartment."

Ever frugal with her money, Katie enthused about the bargains she'd found for their new home. Carrie's comforter, she said, was purchased for 75 percent off at a store in California. These remarks came from the woman who had just signed a new contract with NBC worth $7 million a year.

While the *Good Housekeeping* writer was visiting Katie, the phone rang. It was a U.S. general calling from Germany. He needed to talk to Katie about a possible interview with three U.S. soldiers who had just been released by Serbian military forces after spending more than a month as prisoners of war. In part because of the efforts of the Rev. Jesse Jackson, Serbian authorities freed the men on May 2, 1999, and allowed Staff Sergeant Christopher J. Stone, Staff Sergeant Andrew A. Ramirez, and Specialist Steven M. Gonzales to travel to Ramstein Air Base in Germany. In a moment, Katie easily shifted from

discussing decorating ideas with a reporter to deter-
mining the facts about the American captives with
the general. A journalist at heart, she knew that it
was important to take the call, even if the timing for
it was inconvenient.

When she finished talking with the general, Katie
returned to discussing her new home with Joanna
Powell. Katie explained that one of her favorite
items in the apartment is an antique soldier in
Napoleonic uniform that Jay purchased just a few
weeks before he died. When Jay bought the life-
sized mannequin, Katie thought it looked somewhat
strange with its metal helmet and hip-high black
boots. After Jay's death, Katie did not know what
to do with it. But the interior decorator who
helped with the new apartment suggested she put it
in the dining room where the soldier's red, white,
and blue uniform colors blended nicely with the
blue walls.

The soldier seemed content there, with its eyes
peering out from beneath its helmet, from the corner
of the room. Then one day little Carrie caught Katie
by surprise. "That's Jay," she said, pointing at the
antique soldier. Katie confessed to the *Good Housekeeping* writer that since that moment she has been
perfectly comfortable with the soldier. "I feel like
he's watching over us," she said.

While showing Powell around her new home,
Katie talked about Jay's collection of old brass
bugles and the other artifacts belonging to his Civil
War collection. It was clear to the interviewer that
after the most difficult period of Katie's life, she had
picked up the pieces and was ready to go on. And her
young daughters, Ellie and Carrie, would help.

Throughout the new apartment, memories of Jay
are present. The grand piano that the couple bought
as a present for themselves sits in the living room. If
she tries, Katie said, she can still hear Jay playing the

On June 3, 1999, Katie joined (from left) actor John Leguizamo, hockey great Wayne Gretzky, and basketball star Teresa Weatherspoon in accepting "All American Hero" Awards from the Fresh Air Fund. Katie's excellence as a journalist and her work for people in need have earned her many honors.

ragtime tunes that he so loved. But those memories blend with the sound of Ellie practicing for her piano lessons. Katie, too, snatches moments to play a few tunes—and on occasion sing along.

Helping Ellie and Carrie deal with their father's death is an ongoing challenge. But in the same way as she talks to millions of Americans each day, Katie takes a down-to-earth approach with her daughters. Carrie was only two when her father died, so Katie has had to help her understand what his death really meant. Couric hired a full-time live-in to take care of the girls, but she still spends a lot of time with her daughters. Some friends claim that Katie and the girls have watched every Disney movie that was ever made.

Even though Jay is still very much on her mind, Katie's priorities are her children and her career. Each weekday morning she banters with her *Today* colleagues—Matt, Al, and newsreader Ann Curry— and still enjoys the show's relaxed nature.

Katie remains very popular with television viewers. She was flattered when a national magazine reported that its readers said she would be a good candidate for president, and she laughed on the air one morning when people in the crowd outside the *Today* building waved a flag that read, "Katie for President."

Throughout her career Katie has continued to gather professional awards for her journalistic achievements. She has been honored with a second Emmy Award, a Matrix Award, a National Headliner Award, and the Sigma Delta Chi Award from the Society of Professional Journalists. The *Washington Journalism Review* once named her the "Best in the Business."

In January 1999, *Life* magazine named Katie one of its "Heroes of the Year" for the grace that she showed in the face of Jay's death. *Good Housekeeping* named her the top journalist in its "Most Admired Women Poll" the same month. Later that year, *American Health* magazine named Katie one of its 10 "Women's Health Heroes."

Katie's picture and name regularly pop up in magazine and newspaper articles. In December 1999, *Redbook* magazine reported a list of Katie's "favorite things" alongside a photograph of her and Ellie. The list included "Singing in the shower (or anyplace else!); Bacon cooking on Sunday morning; Group hugs with my daughters; The beach at 5 p.m.; The way you feel after a shower after a day at the beach; Cary Grant."

As part of her ongoing work for NBC, Katie agreed to report on the new millennium celebration. December 31, 1999, was a long Friday for Katie, but her smile

Katie donates both time and money to many charitable causes. In October 1999 she appeared at a gala for the National Osteoporosis Foundation (NOF) with (from left) Senator John Glenn, NOF chairman Paul G. Rogers, and NOF president C. Conrad Johnston, in New York City.

was bright and her spirit cheerful as she rallied in the new year next to old friend Tom Brokaw. Dressed in a black turtleneck sweater and a bright red coat, Katie chatted with Brokaw throughout the evening coverage.

The new millennium brought both changes and opportunities. Two years after Jay's death Katie began dating again. According to a November 2000 *People* magazine article, she dated various men that year, including Los Angeles–based multimillionaire Tom Werner, coproducer of sitcoms such as *The Cosby Show* and *Third Rock from the Sun.* Her new relationships have drawn her into an interesting role reversal. Katie reports that her daughter Ellie acts more like a mother these days, wanting to know what time Katie's going to be home after her date.

New challenges arose for Couric in July 2000 when her older sister, Emily, who had been running for lieutenant governor of Virginia, was diagnosed with pancreatic cancer. She withdrew from the race. Out of respect for her sister, Katie declines to make public comments about the situation, but she continues to raise money for cancer research. Working with Lilly Tartikoff, Katie helped organize and find sponsors for the October 2000 5K run/walk in Washington, D.C., for the National Colorectal Cancer Research Alliance. The event drew thousands of participants and concluded with a free concert by singer/songwriter Paul Simon.

"The most difficult part of Jay's illness," Katie told *Good Housekeeping* writer Joanna Powell during an interview two years after Jay died, "was to see someone you love so much suffer and get gypped out of life. But another really agonizing aspect was how powerless I felt. I'm one of those people who likes to fix things and make everything OK. Even though I tried everything I could, save throwing on a lab coat and becoming a cancer researcher, which I couldn't be because I'm not nearly smart enough, I just couldn't do it. There was nothing I could do to make Jay better. And so assisting other people has been a great antidote for that feeling of helplessness."

Katie also continues to build her career. In the fall of 2000, NBC expanded the *Today* show's time slot by an hour, giving both Katie and Matt time for many more interviews and segments each day. Besides serving as coanchor for *Today*, Couric also is a contributing anchor for the news show *Dateline NBC*. Her efforts were rewarded in February 2001 when she was named Best News Person of the year by *TV Guide*.

While her work occupies much of her time, Katie has still found the opportunity to write a children's book. *The Brand New Kid* features Lazlo, a new boy at school who is from Hungary. In the story, Lazlo

Katie signs a copy of her book, The Brand New Kid, *at an October 19, 2000, book signing at Rockefeller Center in New York City.*

is ignored or teased by the other children because he looks different from them and talks with an accent. Katie hopes the book will start conversations between parents and children and between teachers and students about dealing with differences between people. She is under contract to write two more children's books.

In many ways, it seems as if the old Katie Couric has returned. The spirited anchor had gone through a long healing process, but she has become a wiser, stronger woman because of it. And having watched Katie confront such challenging events on a very public stage, millions of people continue to be inspired by her.

1957   Born to John and Elinor Couric on January 7 in Arlington, Virginia

1975   Graduates from Yorktown High School in Arlington

1979   Receives bachelor's degree with honors from the University of Virginia in Charlottesville; begins working as a desk assistant at the ABC News bureau in Washington, D.C.

1980   Joins CNN at its Washington bureau as an assignment editor

1984   Becomes a general assignment reporter at WTVJ in Miami; wins an award for her series on child pornography

1986   Returns to Washington, D.C., where she becomes a general assignment reporter at WRC-TV, the local NBC television affiliate

1989   Wins a local Emmy Award and an Associated Press Award for her segment about a dating service for the disabled; becomes deputy Pentagon reporter for NBC; marries Jay Monahan

1990   Becomes national correspondent for the *Today* show in New York City

1991   Becomes *Today* show cohost with Bryant Gumbel; gives birth to Elinor Tully Monahan

1992   Covers the Barcelona Olympics and U.S. presidential election; does a 20-minute impromptu interview with President George Bush during a tour of the White House

1993   Becomes coanchor on *Now with Tom Brokaw and Katie Couric*, an evening newsmagazine produced by NBC

1994   *Now* becomes part of *Dateline NBC*; Katie refocuses attention on *Today*; is joined full-time by Jay in New York City

1996   Covers the Olympics in Atlanta and the U.S. presidential campaign; gives birth to Caroline Couric Monahan; *Today* producer Jeff Zucker is diagnosed with and recovers from colon cancer

1997   Is joined on *Today* by coanchor Matt Lauer after the resignation of Bryant Gumbel; husband, Jay Monahan, is diagnosed with colon cancer

1998   Jay Monahan dies of colon cancer; Katie creates colon cancer series for *Today*; cofounds the National Colorectal Cancer Research Alliance

1999   Goes to Littleton, Colorado, to cover the shootings at Columbine High School; is named a "Hero of the Year" by *Life* magazine; becomes the top journalist in *Good Housekeeping*'s "Most Admired Women" poll; is appointed one of 10 "Women's Health Heroes" by *American Health* magazine

2000   *Today* show expands to three hours; Katie's older sister, Emily, develops pancreatic cancer; children's book *The Brand New Kid* is published; covers U.S. presidential campaign

2001   Is named Best News Person of the Year by *TV Guide*

BIBLIOGRAPHY

Books and Periodicals

Bumiller, Elisabeth. "What You Don't Know About Katie Couric." *Good Housekeeping*, August 1996.

Burrelle's Information Services. *Today* Show Transcript, 22 April 1999.

———. *Today* Show Transcript, 29 October 1999.

Burton, Tony. "My Favorite Things." *Redbook*, December 1999.

Couric, Katie. "Travels with Katie Couric." *National Geographic Traveler*, November 1994.

"Dance Fever." *People*, 27 May 1996.

DePaulo, Lisa. "Killer Katie." *George*, May 1997.

Diamond, Edwin. "The Couric Effect." *New York Magazine*, 9 December 1991.

Flander, Judy. "Catching Up with Katie Couric." *Saturday Evening Post*, September/October 1992.

Gliatto, Tom. "With Deborah Norville switched to the mommy track, *Today* has arrived for new coanchor Katie Couric." *People*, 22 April 1991.

Grove, Lloyd. "Kiss of the Anchorwoman." *Vanity Fair*, August 1994.

Hack, Richard. *Madness in the Morning*. Beverly Hills, Calif.: New Millennium Press, 1999.

Johnson, Peter. "Couric Returns with Grace, Then Gets Right to Work." *USA Today*, 25 February 1998.

"Katie Couric." *People*, 28 December 1992.

Kaufman, Joanne. "Katie Couric Today." *TV Guide*, 6 February 1993.

Kelley, Courtney. "I Knew I Was Turning into a Mother When . . ." *Glamour*, May 1994.

Krupp, Charla. "The Today Show's Katie Couric." *Glamour*, July 1991.

———. "Dressing for Two: Katie Couric's Maternity Dilemma." *InStyle*, 1 January 1996.

Langford, Bob. "Triangle Airwaves—Is Katie Here Today, Gone Tomorrow." *Raleigh (N.C.) News & Observer*, 17 April 1991.

Lampert, Leslie "Katie's Place." *Ladies Home Journal*, May 1994.

Levine, Daniel R., compiler. "My First Job." *Reader's Digest*, January 1995.

McClellan, Steve. "Katie Stays at *Today*." *Broadcasting & Cable*, 6 July 1998.

McElwaine, Sandra. "A Fresh Look at Katie Couric." *USA Weekend*, 25 April 1993.

Marin, Rick. "He Was Everything I Look For." *Newsweek*, 6 July 1998.

Marin, Rick, and Yahlin Chang. "The Katie Factor." *Newsweek*, 6 July 1998.

"NBC *Today* Interview with First Lady Barbara Bush." Federal News Service Washington Package, 13 October 1992. (Available from Dow Jones Interactive Publication Library.)

Petrucelli, Alan W. "Down-to-Earth Katie Couric." *Working Mother*, July–August, 1996.

Powell, Joanna. "Katie's Crusade." *Good Housekeeping*, October 1998.

———. "Katie's Haven." *Good Housekeeping*, September 1999.

———. "Katie's New Life." *Good Housekeeping*, November 2000.

"Prior to Arrival." *People*, 3 July 1995.

Roberts, Roxanne. "Yipes! It's Katie Couric!—Don't Call Her Cute or Perky. Just Call Her '*Today*'s Hope for Tomorrow.'" *Washington Post*, 21 May 1991.

Rohde, David. "Jay Monahan is Dead at 42." *New York Times*, 26 January 1998.

Romano, Lois. "Stories That Changed Their Lives." *Redbook*, October 1991.

Schwarzbaum, Lisa. "Katie Couric's Charm Sparks *Today* Comeback." *Richmond (Virginia) Times-Dispatch*, 30 July 1992.

———. "Katie Did It." *Entertainment Weekly*, 31 July 1992.

Weber, Bruce. "At Home with Katie Couric." *New York Times*, 9 April 1992.

"Winners of the Most Admired Women Poll." *Good Housekeeping*, January 1999.

"Women's Health Heroes." *American Health*, October 1999.

Websites

"Colorectal Cancer." InteliHealth. *http://www.intelihealth.com*

"The Essential Katie Couric Collection." *http://members.aol.com.flopez1541/*

"Katie Couric." MSNBC. *http://www.msnbc.com/onair/bios/k_couric.asp*

INDEX

INDEX

PICTURE CREDITS ═══════

Sherry Beck Paprocki is an award-winning journalist who has written for the *Chicago Tribune*, the *Philadelphia Inquirer*, the *Cleveland Plain Dealer*, the *Los Angeles Times Syndicate*, and many other publications. Her first children's book, *Easy Microwave Cooking for Kids*, was published in 1987. Since then she has written or contributed to five other books for children and adults, including *Michelle Kwan*, a biography published by Chelsea House. A graduate of Ohio State University, she resides in Granville, Ohio, with her husband, who is also a writer, and their two children.

Matina S. Horner was president of Radcliffe College and associate professor of psychology and social relations at Harvard University. She is best known for her studies of women's motivation, achievement, and personality development. Dr. Horner has served on several national boards and advisory councils, including those of the National Science Foundation, Time Inc., and the Women's Research and Education Institute. She earned her B.A. from Bryn Mawr College and her Ph.D. from the University of Michigan, and holds honorary degrees from many colleges and universities, including Mount Holyoke, Smith, Tufts, and the University of Pennsylvania.